Medieval Imagery
in Today's Politics

PAST IMPERFECT

Past Imperfect presents concise critical overviews of the latest research by the world's leading scholars. Subjects cross the full range of fields in the period ca. 400—1500 CE which, in a European context, is known as the Middle Ages. Anyone interested in this period will be enthralled and enlightened by these overviews, written in provocative but accessible language. These affordable paperbacks prove that the era still retains a powerful resonance and impact throughout the world today.

Director and Editor-in-Chief
Simon Forde, *'s-Hertogenbosch*

Acquisitions Editors
Erin Dailey, *Leeds*
Ruth Kennedy, *Adelaide*

Production
Ruth Kennedy, *Adelaide*

Cover Design
Linda K. Judy, *Michigan*

Medieval Imagery in Today's Politics

Daniel Wollenberg

Library of Congress Cataloging in Publication Data

A catalogue record for this book is available from the Library of Congress.

© 2018, Arc Humanities Press, Leeds

Printed and bound by CPI Group (UK) Ltd, Croydon, CR0 4YY

ISBN (print): 9781942401407
eISBN (PDF): 9781942401414
eISBN (EPUB): 9781942401421

arc-humanitiespress.org

Contents

Acknowledgements

Thanks very much to Simon Forde and Ruth Kennedy for getting the exciting Past Imperfect series off the ground and helping guide this book through to publication.

For their encouragement, conviviality, and common sense, much gratitude is due to my colleagues at the University of Tampa in the English and Writing Department and beyond, especially to David Reamer, for being a good friend and department chair, and to Dan Dooghan, Sarah Juliet Lauro, Kacy Tillman, and Joe Letter for helping me clarify and hone ideas in our reading group. I was able to conduct certain parts of the research here due to grants and conference funding from the University of Tampa, for which I am grateful. To my students: thanks for keeping me on my toes.

I would also like to thank my friends and colleagues at conferences, particularly the Middle Ages in the Modern World, who have helped shape my thoughts and have challenged me, especially to my "panel comrades" Andrew Elliott and Mike Evans.

For the many wonderful years of love, patience, support, laughter, source hunting, and matzo ball soup: thanks, Leslie. This book, like everything that I do, is for you.

Introduction

The Past Awakening

In the middle of the afternoon on May 21, 2013, a 78 year-old historian walked up to the altar in the Notre-Dame Cathedral in Paris, pulled out a pistol, and shot himself in the mouth. Dominique Venner, a white-nationalist extremist whose writings range from eleven volumes on the history of firearms to an apologia for the Vichy regime to a survey of the traditions of "Europeans" over the last 30,000 years, meant for his very public suicide to be a symbolic protestation against the destruction of racial, national, and cultural identity. In a suicide note left on the Notre Dame altar, Venner denounced the unmooring of the "anchors of our identity" and hoped for a future rebirth of ancestral French and European values. The goal of his final act was to kindle the race consciousness of his fellow Frenchmen and Europeans, so that like him, they might see with clear eyes that a cathedral like Notre-Dame was built by "the genius of my ancestors" and perceive a communal European memory stretching back to Homer. For five decades, Venner had argued for the paramount importance of a white heritage and ancestry that give people's lives shape and meaning. On the day of his suicide, Marine Le Pen, the nationalist leader of the French far-right political party *Front National*, tweeted, "All our respect to Dominique Venner, whose last gesture ... had been to try to wake the people of France."[1] Venner's suicide, meant as an alarm for the sleeping race-blind, seems primarily to have shaken those who were already awake.

Among the "awoken"—in this case, the far and extreme right in North America and Western Europe—the intense and pervasive belief that communities of place, people, and nation have been seriously eroded in the last few decades has caused a retreat back into identity. In Europe over the last decade, increasing immigration from the Middle East and Africa, combined with nearly a dozen major terrorist attacks between 2010 and 2017, have bolstered a populist right that often whispers—and sometimes openly and vehemently advocates—xenophobic and Islamophobic rhetoric. With the rise of ethnic nationalism has come a heightened attention to defining authentic Americanness and Frenchness and Europeanness and, in turn, whiteness. At the core of that ethnic nationalism is the association of modernity with liberalism, tolerance, individualism, and multiculturalism; and of the premodern—the medieval—with solidarity, stability, law and order, cultural advance, and security.

In the United States, the American presidential election of 2016 revealed a serious crisis of white identity. What was once extremist or far-right thought now is discussed openly in mainstream venues and is alluded to, in however sugarcoated a way, in some of Donald Trump's, and his advisors', own discourse. That discourse at times draws on the medieval past, whether to paint enemies as primitive savages (which Trump himself often does) or to give weight to claims for the longevity and legitimacy of a unified white culture that has been battling for its survival for centuries (as his former chief strategist Steve Bannon has done). "If you look back at the long history of the Judeo-Christian West struggle against Islam," Bannon said in an interview at the Vatican in 2014, "I believe that our forefathers kept their stance, and I think they did the right thing. I think they kept it out of the world, whether it was at Vienna, or Tours, or other places ... it bequeathed to us the great institution that is the church of the West."[2] This interview posits a permanent clash of civilizations between the Christian West and the Islamic East. "Our forefathers" are those who fought against Islamic forces at the Battle of Tours in 732 and against the Turks at the Siege of Vienna in 1529, digging in their heels and standing up to defend European values. Bannon finished the interview with dire warnings about the "Judeo-Christian" battle with Islam and more praise for "our forefathers" who "bequeath[ed] to us a church and a civilization that really is the flower of mankind." The implication is that the West's strongest institutions and values, rooted in the Middle Ages, are under assault today as they were in the medieval past. This is white identity under siege. What was once boilerplate fodder for extremist white nationalists has become part of mainstream discourse.

Two opposing views of the medieval in political rhetoric—as the diabolical primitive and as the bedrock of modern identity—are studied here. The primary aim of this short book is not to set the record straight on the medieval. A medievalist could spend a whole career correcting common falsehoods about the Middle Ages and still not make much progress convincing anybody of the textures of an "authentic" or "real" Middle Ages, as opposed to the fabricated Middle Ages concocted so often by political rhetoric or in popular culture. This is because in many ways the medieval is a modern chimera. The medieval was constructed when post-Renaissance modernity moulded and solidified it into a mirror and contrast of what the modern was not.

While each of the simplifications and misrepresentations and misreadings of the Middle Ages, from dark medievalism to neo-feudalism to an organic and homogeneous white Middle Ages, clearly deserve their own full rebuttal, this short book is not quite the place where that work can be done. The primary aim of this book is, more simply, to introduce how and why the premodern past is manipulated and deployed as a means to certain political ends today. The first chapter introduces the medieval as an inherently politically charged concept in contemporary political discourse and examines dark medievalism in particular. The second chapter then turns to the far and extreme right's association of white identity with the Middle Ages at the more radical ends of political discourse. The third chapter examines Traditionalist Conservatism in the US and Europe, showing how the far- and extreme-right's embrace of medieval cultural heritage has been central to certain strands of relatively mainstream conservative thought for decades, if not longer. The fourth chapter turns its attention to political medievalism on the left (though not exclusively the left) and in the academy by considering the concept of "neo-feudalism" and revisiting the New Medievalism of International Relations theory. At the end of the book, there is a Further Reading section that offers selected texts beyond those cited in the endnotes.

A decade ago, Bruce Holsinger wrote a short but essential book on terrorism, politics, and medievalism called *Neomedievalism, Neoconservatism, and the War on Terror*, which remains vital reading for anyone interested in how political discourse in the post-9/11 years consistently drew on the medieval to give shape to present uncertainties. Since that book's publication, the Middle Ages have become increasingly central to the politics of cultural and ethnic identity on the far right and to explanations by the left for increasing injustice and inequality. Holsinger suggested that in the toxic political environment that existed after 9/11, medievalists' good intentions might be mis-construed as defending terrorists. That seems less likely today—although with the election of Donald Trump, per-haps I am being overly optimistic. Medievalists—scholars who specialize in the study of the Middle Ages—ought not to demand that the Middle Ages be completely excised from political discourse. If people with a public voice think the Middle Ages are important, then we should seize that opportunity to examine how the past can be exploited for political purchase.

Notes

[1] "Tout notre respect à Dominique Venner dont le dernier geste, éminemment politique, aura été de tenter de réveiller le peuple de France. MLP," Marine Le Pen, Twitter post, May 21, 2013, 12:14 p.m., https://twitter.com/mlp_officiel/status/336877763183140864 (my translation).

[2] J. Lester Feder, "This Is how Steve Bannon Sees the Entire World," *Buzzfeed*, November 15, 2016, https://www.buzzfeed.com/lesterfeder/this-is-how-steve-bannon-sees-the-entire-world?utm_term=.hllqE9vvv#.kug78KJJJ (accessed December 1, 2016).

Chapter 1

Getting Political

When Thomas Fosbroke coined the adjective "medieval" in 1817, he may not have intended it to be political—and yet it is.

Whether we are discussing *media tempestas* (coined in 1469), *medium tempus* (1534), or *medium aevum* (1604), the Middle Ages intrinsically mean an intervening period of time between classical antiquity and the present day.[3] This middle period was meant to be the inverse of other periods: it was not the Renaissance and it was not modern.

The existence of the medieval as an idea requires, of course, another political idea: the *rinascita*—the rebirth, the Renaissance. Like so many modern concepts and phrases that work to periodize history, the word "Renaissance" was projected backwards onto a distant past. For Jules Michelet, who coined the term in 1855, the Renaissance represented a progressive, democratic condition that celebrated the same virtues of Reason and Truth that he valued. Michelet was a French nationalist. Although he traced the seeds of a unified French nation and national spirit to the twelfth, thirteenth, and fourteenth centuries and admired medieval heroes of the French people like Joan of Arc, on the whole Michelet projected tyranny, oppression, and disunity onto the Middle Ages and freedom, democracy, and justice onto the Renaissance.[4] The very notion of the Renaissance was political at its core and it in turn politicized the medieval.

Even if Fosbroke intended for "medieval" to be a neutral term, as opposed to the loaded "feudal" and "Gothic," the medieval is certainly political now. Donald Trump regularly excites and frightens audiences with pictures of atavistic violence happening in a nebulous East, deflecting lines of attack against him by telling us about what truly matters. This is no time for critiquing his "tone" because "when you have people that are cutting Christians' heads off, when you have a world ... [in which] it is medieval times ... it almost has to be as bad as it ever was in terms of the violence and the horror."[5] As bad as it ever was. This is the eternal medieval, a medieval that defies chronological and geographical boundaries. Far from being a simple cop-out for deflecting criticism of his tone, Trump has repeatedly returned to the theme of medieval decapitation, usually for a more nefarious purpose than simply deflecting criticism of his vocal delivery: "In the Middle East, we have people chopping the heads off Christians, we have people chopping the heads off many other people. We have things that we have never seen before ... The medieval times, I mean, we studied medieval times—not since medieval times have people seen what's going on. I would bring back waterboarding and I'd bring back a hell of a lot worse than waterboarding."[6] A round of applause from the crowd followed this confused polemic. The medieval is not a discrete historical period for Trump. It is something both new and old: both unprecedented and yet also an archaic and permanent threat. It is at once novel and a relic from the uncivilized past. Trump's medieval is a state of being. It always was and, without an apt and equal response of American action, always will be. This action includes torture, which he considers a "medieval" course of action but a crucial last resort for achieving victory over premodern foes. But any American response, however severe, cannot be "medieval," because it will be conducted by an advanced, modern nation. One wonders who the "we" is that has studied medieval times.

Perhaps that student of the medieval is Carly Fiorina, a one-time rival of Trump's for the Republican Party's Presidential nomination in 2016. A former corporate executive with a BA in philosophy and medieval history from Stanford, Fiorina seemed delighted to discover that her undergraduate degree from one of the best universities in the world was suddenly useful. Why? Because her academic study of the Middle Ages could help her understand the medieval practices and medieval society of the Islamic State. She promised her supporters at a New England rally in 2015 that her degree in medieval history was a valuable asset because "what ISIS wants to do is drive us back to the Middle Ages, literally."[7] The "literally" is the give-away—her way of insinuating that she has concrete scholarly knowledge of the Middle Ages and is not being merely metaphorical here. Fiorina's medieval is the real medieval, not the greasy pageantry of American theme restaurants or zingers from a Tarantino film. Islamic State deals in the literal medieval. For Fiorina, torture and brutality are the ghosts of the medieval: "Every single one of the techniques that ISIS is using, the crucifixion, the beheadings, the burning alive, those were commonly used techniques in the Middle Ages." Driving home the point, Fiorina insisted that "ISIS wants to take its territory back to the Middle Ages," and that we would be naïve and foolish to charge her with exaggeration on this front. Like Trump, Fiorina uses bad history and bad logic to defend the necessity of torture: they do it, so we must, too.

Bruce Holsinger was absolutely right to call Fiorina's absurd medievalism "a failure of historical imagination" for its inaccuracy about torture and execution practices in the Middle Ages and its misreading of the Islamic State as inherently medieval, rather than seeing them as exploiters of social media and mass communication.[8] Fiorina's triumvirate of beheadings, crucifixion, and burnings emanates from a mainstream discourse about the "medieval" nature of ISIS, which contends that they are the real-deal re-enactors of early Islamic practices and the literal word of the Qu'ran. In a 2015 *Atlantic* article by Graeme Wood, Bernard Haykel, a scholar of Near Eastern Studies, gave scholarly legitimacy to Wood's argument that ISIS has an authentically "medieval religious nature."[9] Haykel draws on a similar medieval torture triumvirate as Fiorina, insisting that "[s]lavery, crucifixion, and beheadings are not something that freakish [jihadists] are cherry-picking from the medieval tradition." Islamic State fighters, for Haykel, "are smack in the middle of the medieval tradition and are bringing it wholesale into the present day." As with Fiorina, Haykel insists on the literal medieval of the Islamic State.

The conception of a Dark Ages, though definitively repudiated by historians for at least the last half-century, persists in the dark medievalism of collective memory. The dark medievalism of the dystopian primitive is on full display in histrionic books that warn readers about impending relapses into nebulous pasts that never really existed. The titles of Morris Berman's *Dark Ages America* or Jane Jacobs's *Dark Age Ahead*, both published during the second Bush administration, are not simply idiomatic. Berman draws explicit connections between the "Dark or Middle Ages" and the United States in the early twenty-first century.[10] Some characteristically dark medieval elements that now plague America are garden-variety misconceptions about the period between Roman antiquity and the Enlightenment: the triumph of religion over reason; the decline of critical thinking; and, of course, the predominance of torture. Berman all but admits that his history is bad history. While gesturing towards the fact that scholarship over the last half-century has dismissed the quality of darkness as being useful or accurate for describing the early Middle Ages, he then brushes this scholarship away by reassuring us that dark "is the operative word" (2). Berman nearly— but not totally—comes clean in his implicit suggestions that actual history does not really matter. Here we return to the problem of torture. Torture, Berman writes, "evokes the culture of the Dark and Middle Ages" (7) more than anything else. Our collective memory about the period remembers it as a barbaric time and the medieval torture chamber is our enduring image of that past. Berman is in effect admitting here that his depiction of the Middle Ages is based entirely on popular (mis)conceptions. No matter; all that counts is the utility of the image. Whereas Trump and Fiorina invoke "medieval" torture in order to argue that America needs to combat fundamentalist primitivism, Berman's account of American torture differs by using medievality to condemn the Bush administration as cruel, barbaric, atavistic, and un-American. Both approaches utilize the medieval as a political tool.

Dark medievalism is not a uniquely American phenomenon. Egregious abuses of dark medievalism as a political tool have been performed by Israeli Prime Minister Benjamin Netanyahu, who has attempted to delegitimize his state's enemies by invoking a chronological struggle for survival. Netanyahu's historiography is a make-believe fantasy where the misty biblical past, for which there are few historical records to corroborate his account, is lionized, but the medieval past, for which there is an abundance of tangible records, is disparaged. The Prime Minister's words are worth quoting at some length:

> In Israel, the past and the future find common ground. Unfortunately, that is not the case in many other countries.

For today, a great battle is being waged between the modern and the medieval. The forces of modernity seek a bright future in which the rights of all are protected, in which an ever-expanding digital library is available in the palm of every child, in which every life is sacred. The forces of medievalism seek a world in which women and minorities are subjugated, in which knowledge is suppressed, in which not life but death is glorified. These forces clash around the globe, but nowhere more starkly than in the Middle East. Israel stands proudly with the forces of modernity ... [Militant Islamists] want to drag humanity back to an age of unquestioning dogma and unrelenting conflict ... Ultimately, light will penetrate the darkness. We've seen that happen before. Some five hundred years ago, the printing press helped pry a cloistered Europe out of a dark age. Eventually, ignorance gave way to enlightenment.[11]

Here is dark medievalism in its full glory. This speech was given to the United Nations in September 2012, occasioned by a warning about the uranium enrichment capabilities of Iran. The "facts" that Netanyahu presented amounted, more or less, to a simplistic and crudely drawn bomb, which looked like a water balloon, in order to demonstrate how far Iran had come in its nuclear-bomb-making abilities. The urgent red flag that the Prime Minister was hoisting was the need to stop Iran from destroying Israel. Militant Islamists and the state of Iran were conflated to mean the exact same thing. The lack of nuance in distinguishing between the leaders of Iran and jihadists led to a clear implication: Israel stands for modernity and its enemies, in all forms, stand for medievality. This medievality—its brutal violence, subjugation of women, death culture, and denial of rational thought—is characteristic of militant Islamists, including Iran. Medievality is cured by modernity, which will make the medieval Muslims "yield to the irresistible power of freedom and technology." Netanyahu was not careful in his choice of words, implying that the entire region outside of Israel is comprised of conspiratorial fantasists, as opposed to the rational, intellectual, thoroughly modern state of Israel.

He could not denigrate and cast off the whole premodern past, though, because it is that past that legitimizes, for Netanyahu, Israel's right to exist. "The clash between modernity and medievalism need not be a clash between progress and tradition," the Prime Minister concluded. The millennia-old traditions of the Jewish people cause them to have, rather than stymie them from having, a progressive attitude towards the future. Samuel Huntingdon's controversial and highly problematic interpretation of the "clash of civilizations" theory, which posits that there exists, and has long existed, a gap between West and East that cannot be bridged, here morphs into a clash between the modern and the medieval. "Medievalism" stands in for all of the past that Netanyahu does not like. The biblical Jewish past serves as a teleological prelude to the modern state of Israel, whereas the medieval past of radical Islamists is the exact same as their present, as they endlessly spin their wheels in the medieval mud. "We and they" becomes "present and past." History is co-opted into an account that fits Israel's political needs, both justifying the right of the state to exist and their right to use violence against its enemies.

The dark medievalism trope persists beyond rightwing politicians in Israel and the United States. Dark medievalism is not a solely right-wing phenomenon, nor is the right a homogenous entity in their beliefs about the Middle Ages. The left has historically relied heavily on a narrative of chronological and ideological progression, of moving beyond the past and dismantling tradition. Some on the left also give voice to dark medievalism. Former American Secretary of State John Kerry hedged his bets by describing radical Islamists as both "medieval and modern fascism at the same time," insinuating the common right-wing rallying cry of Islamofascism while lumping together all of America's enemies in the world wars and today into the same pot.[12]

The paradigm of a West that has moved beyond the primitive and incessantly marches in progress towards a greater degree of civilization, away from the uncivilized past, forms the core of an orientalist mindset that seeks dominion over territories, minds, and wallets. In Said's account of orientalism, European culture is depicted as and assumed to be superior to non-European cultures, and the Orient is constructed in theory and practice as backward and primitive. Western society is rational and progressive while the East is irrational and atavistic, enabling cultural and political domination of them. John Ganim has insightfully connected medievalism with orientialism by showing how medievalism functions like orientialism; just as the Eastern other is constructed as being exotic and culturally underdeveloped in the orientalist mindset, the medieval is constructed as a prior and less civilized stage of cultural and political development in the medievalist mindset. According to Ganim, as the Middle Ages came to be an object of fascination in the eighteenth century, they "represented in time what the Orient represented in space, an 'other' to the present development of Western civilization."[13] As Clare Monagle and Louise D'Arcens have argued, removing the enemy from the present and placing them in the medieval past renders them as primitive, barbaric, and irrational. The important and perceptive point that Monagle and D'Arcens make is that medievalizing radical Islamists ultimately works to justify their permanent imprisonment and torture, because those combatants operating outside of the traditional nation-state system are not covered by the rules of engagement applied to traditional enemies acting on behalf of a state.[14] Medievalizing the enemy legitimizes "medieval"-style practices that may be used to thwart them.

A number of commentaries have appeared over the last few years in response to the numerous exhortations of Islamic State as medieval savages, insisting that politicians, whatever their political stripe, not blatantly manipulate history so wilfully. Most of these commentaries are well-intentioned correctives tending to attempt to correct popular misconceptions about the medieval by insisting that political rhetoric in general avoid the term altogether. The argument that some commenters have made is that Islamic State is actually thoroughly modern, steeped in technology as well as in a modern political framework, as the notion of an Islamic state is crafted in the mould of post-Westphalian nation states. The very act of calling Islamic State medieval accedes to and legitimizes the story that they want to tell about themselves, argues Kevin McDonald, as Islamic State tries to spin a narrative of being the true, authentic Islamists who are trying to recreate the conditions of medieval Islam and the medieval Middle East.[15] One important insight from these editorials has been that, like many in the West, Islamic State also evokes a fantasy medieval past. Islamic State wants to be seen as anti-Crusaders, as did bin Laden; they constantly evoke crusader language in their manifesto "The Management of Savagery" and consistently refer to Westerners as Crusaders. Historian John Terry argues that Islamic State itself is "nostalgic for a make-believe past."[16] When Islamic State refers to Islam's seventh-century conquests, they draw on a reading of history that glorifies a holy conquest over infidels; like some politicians and presidential candidates, they are bad historians, revising history without understanding or caring about more nuanced narratives of the period, early Islam, and the Prophet. According to Terry, the Islamic State misremembers history.

The Crusades have become a flashpoint of bad history used to make a political argument. Susan Jacoby, for instance, was not wrong in her *New York Times* editorial piece when she refers to medieval crusaders seeking religious and political power through violence.[17] But this relatively straightforward proposition, that medieval crusaders committed acts of violence in the name of their religion, is warped by Jacoby into "a standard of medieval behavior" that demonstrates "what the Western world might look like had there never been religious reformations, the Enlightenment and, above all, the separation of church and state." Radical Islamists are thus both memory and warning: what once was and what could still be.

There is, of course, nothing particularly Islamic—or Christian or Jewish, for that matter—about atrocity, violence, and power. Barack Obama attempted to make this point, albeit in an indirect (and largely ineffective) way, in his controversial National Prayer Breakfast speech in 2015. Obama chastised Christians at the breakfast for condemning Islamic violence when they themselves have their own history of violence, setting off a wave of angry conservative reactions, the majority of which took issue with his chastisement of Christians rather than Muslims, the real culprits. Obama's crime was implying that triumphalism, jingoism, and xenophobia are not productive and are inconsistent with American ideals. The former president "offended every believing Christian in the United States" and "does not believe in America," cried former Virginia governor Jim Gilmore, with the subtext of sketching Obama as a foreign other sympathetic with the nation's enemies.[18] Here is a portion of this most offensive statement made by Obama: "[L]est we get on our high horse and think [violence in the name of religion] is unique to some other place, remember that during the Crusades and the Inquisition, people committed terrible deeds in the name of Christ."[19] These fairly innocuous comments, which in themselves merely suggest that religious violence is not unique to Islam, and moreover, actually do not differ much from what many Crusade historians have said about the Crusades, ignited a firestorm of vitriol from the right. One particularly vocal commenter on the issue, Thomas Madden, a historian who has written extensively on the Crusades, lambasted Obama for misconstruing history. Not that the Crusaders didn't commit acts of violence; they did, but primarily because they were pushed to do so by an encroaching Islam.

Madden's scholarship on the Crusades espouses a political agenda that recovers and reclaims the Crusades from what he considers a false, leftist interpretation that has persisted for a half-century. In an editorial in *The National Review* that encapsulates his larger argument about the Crusades, Madden reprimanded Obama for purporting to be able to see into the hearts of men, to judge whether their piety is authentic or not, whether they are medieval warriors or modern jihadists. The Crusades, according to Madden, were not a perversion of Christian belief, but defensive wars whose primary purpose was "to save Christian people and restore Christian lands."[20] Applying this logic to Islamic State, politicians cannot know what is in the hearts of modern jihadists, and politicians are not in a position to judge the piety or perversions of their faith. Are Islamic terrorists authentic recreators of seventh-century warriors, or are they thoroughly modern? We cannot tell. The important point for Madden is to sever any link between the Crusades and Islamic State, and the medieval and the modern worlds as a whole. Even if he purports to toe a diplomatic line in the *National Review*, Madden has earlier declared that his version of the Crusades—as defensive wars fought by authentically pious Christian soldiers—is the "real history of the Crusades." In his 2015 article for the *National Review* about Obama and the Crusades, Madden wants to leave the Middle Ages off the table of political discourse, but he had earlier claimed it a "fact that the world we know today would not exist without [Crusaders'] efforts."[21] The medieval past is only off the table when it is put to a political purpose that does not adhere to a particular narrative.

The larger point that I am making here is that the past is in the eye of its beholder. For historians on the right (whether armchair or academic), Obama misreads history by not understanding that the Crusades were provoked by Islamic aggression, were fought by pious Christian warriors, and that they ought not to be used as an antecedent or comparison to the present at all. For historians more to the left, the focus is on Islamic radicals that misread the Crusades for propagandistic purposes and draw ahistorical parallels between the medieval past and the modern present. For both camps, the problem is the bad history of their opponents.

Simply declaring that non-specialists are wrong when they engage in dark medievalism and trying to clarify the *real* medieval does not quite get to the core of the problem, though. Why do we seem to need the medieval brutal, the medieval violent, the medieval atrocity? Why is the medieval so easily politicized today? What accounts for the ubiquity of the dark medieval? Why is the medieval such a useful metaphor? Why, in the words of John Terry, do we "refuse to confront our own nostalgia"? It is certainly true that dark medievalism attempts "to impose chronological distance between ourselves and the things we find unpleasant," as David M. Perry has argued.[22] But it is also true that the medieval has always been modern. This argument lies at the heart of this book. By this I do not mean simply that the concept of the medieval was only defined in the postmedieval period, though this is obviously true.

I mean that the medieval has always been modern in the way that Bruno Latour frames the modern: as an inherent argument for conquest and emancipation from the past. The modern implies a break from (in Latour's words) "an archaic and stable past."[23] The modern thus necessitates essentializing, simplifying, and petrifying the medieval.

Notes

[3] David Matthews, "Middle," in *Medievalism: Key Critical Terms*, ed. Elizabeth Emery and Richard Utz (Cambridge: Brewer, 2014), pp. 141–47.

[4] Stephen A. Kippur, *Jules Michelet: A Study of Mind and Sensibility* (Albany: State University of New York Press, 1981), pp. 79–80.

[5] https://www.washingtonpost.com/news/post-politics/wp/2015/08/06/annotated-transcript-the-aug-6-gop-debate/?utm_term=.cdab1e5ac047 (accessed August 8, 2015).

[6]   http://www.presidency.ucsb.edu/ws/index.php?pid=111472 (accessed February 10, 2016).

[7] Jordyn Phelps, "Carly Fiorina Says Knowledge of Medieval History Will Help her Defeat ISIS," *ABC News*, October 15, 2015, http://abcnews.go.com/Politics/carly-fiorina-medieval-history-degree-helps-defeat-isis/story?id=34256597 (accessed June 5, 2016).

[8] Bruce Holsinger, "Carly Fiorina Goes Medieval," *New York Times*, October 8, 2015, http://www.nytimes.com/2015/10/08/opinion/carly-fiorina-goes-medieval.html?_r=0 (accessed June 5, 2016).

[9] Graeme Wood, "What ISIS Really Wants," *The Atlantic*, March 2015, http://www.theatlantic.com/magazine/archive/2015/03/what-isis-really-wants/384980/ (accessed January 15, 2016).

[10] Morris Berman, *Dark Ages America: The Final Phase of Empire* (New York: W. W. Norton, 2006), p. 1.

[11] http://www.algemeiner.com/2012/09/27/full-transcript-prime-minister-netanyahu-speech-to-united-nations-general-assembly-2012-video/ (accessed September 5, 2013).

[12] Justin Fishel, "John Kerry Equates ISIS Leaders to Fascist Enemies of World Wars," *ABC News*, November 12, 2015, http://abcnews.go.com/International/john-kerry-equates-isis-leaders-fascist-enemies-world/story?id=35152462 (accessed June 11, 2016).

[13] John Ganim, *Medievalism and Orientalism* (New York: Palgrave Macmillan, 2008), p. 85.

[14] Clare Monagle and Louise D'Arcens, "'Medieval' Makes a Comeback in Modern Politics: What's Going On?", *The Conversation*, September 22, 2014, http://theconversation.com/medieval-makes-a-comeback-in-modern-politics-whats-going-on-31780 (accessed June 1, 2016).

[15] Kevin McDonald, "Islamic State's 'Medieval' Ideology Owes a Lot to Revolutionary France," *The Conversation*, September 8, 2014, https://theconversation.com/islamic-states-medieval-ideology-owes-a-lot-to-revolutionary-france-31206 (accessed June 13, 2016).

[16] John Terry, "Why ISIS Isn't Medieval," *Slate*, February 19, 2015, http://www.slate.com/articles/news_and_politics/history/2015/02/isis_isn_t_medieval_its_revisionist_history_only_claims_to_be_rooted_in.html (accessed June 2, 2016).

[17] Susan Jacoby, "The First Victims of the First Crusade," *New York Times*, February 13, 2015, https://www.nytimes.com/2015/02/15/opinion/sunday/the-first-victims-of-the-first-crusade.html (accessed April 5, 2016).

[18] Juliet Eilperin, "Critics Pounce after Obama Talks Crusades, Slavery at Prayer Breakfast," *Washington Post*, February 5, 2015, https://www.washingtonpost.com/politics/obamas-speech-at-prayer-breakfast-called-offensive-to-christians/2015/02/05/6a15a240-ad50-11e4-ad71-7b9eba0f87d6_story.html (accessed June 13, 2016).

[19] https://www.whitehouse.gov/the-press-office/2015/02/05/remarks-president-national-prayer-breakfast (accessed June 20, 2016).

[20] Thomas Madden, "Getting Medieval," *National Review*, February 7, 2015, http://www.nationalreview.com/article/398140/getting-medieval-thomas-f-madden (accessed June 13, 2016).

[21] Thomas Madden, "The Real History of the Crusades," *Crisis Magazine*, March 19, 2011, http://www.crisismagazine.com/2011/the-real-history-of-the-crusades (accessed June 14, 2016).

[22] David M. Perry, "No, Carly Fiorina, a Degree in Medieval History Doesn't Qualify you to Fight ISIS," *The Guardian*, October 6, 2015, https://www.theguardian.com/commentisfree/2015/oct/06/carly-fiorina-medieval-history-degree-fight-isis (accessed June 6, 2016).

[23] Bruno Latour, *We Have Never Been Modern*, trans. Catherine Porter (Cambridge, MA: Harvard University Press, 1993), p. 10.

Chapter 2

Extremes: The Middle Ages on the Fringe

If some political discourse makes a case for the dark medievalism of the foreign enemy, other strands of political discourse, especially but not exclusively on the far fringe of the right, glorify the medieval as the crucial foundation of modern identity. Both ways of utilizing the medieval—as an emblem of brutality and as the root bed of authentic culture and traditions—ossify and embalm the medieval. The Middle Ages as a static incubator of national, ethnic, and racial heritage has proliferated among the politically extreme.

In the six years since Anders Breivik killed 77 Norwegians in the name of an anti-immigrant, anti-leftist, Islamophobic agenda, ethnic nationalism has increased in fervour far beyond Norway. Although he explicitly disavowed neo-Nazism and white supremacy, Breivik's thought was mired in the swamps of such hatred. Claiming to have been motivated by the loss of his Norwegian and Western European identity and culture, Breivik attacked governmental buildings to harm those he perceived as responsible for surrendering his "indigenous" culture. The majority of his victims were wounded and killed during a subsequent attack on the same day on the island of Utøya, at a summer camp run by the Workers Youth League. His victims were teenagers whom he saw as the next generation of leftist multiculturalists who would perpetuate the same surrender of Norway's native white culture as their parents. His attacks were carried out under the flag of the Knights Templar.

Breivik prided himself on being a new incarnation of a Knight Templar, and his manifesto, *2083: A European Declaration of Independence*, digitally self-distributed on the day of the attacks, is rife with engagements with the medieval. Some of the more high-profile discussions of Breivik, such as Åsne Seierstad's book-length study of Breivik and Karl Ove Knausgaard's essay in the *New Yorker*, dismiss Breivik's medievalism as little more than a superficial and immature manifestation of his online avatars in *World of Warcraft*. Despite it being a major aspect of his manifesto, Seierstad barely discusses Breivik's claim to be a new Knight Templar, noting almost in passing the court psychologists' opinion that the network was entirely fabricated, which she accepts without discussion. For Knausgaard, the fantasy of Breivik's online life in *World of Warcraft* came to dominate his reality, enabling him to become "a knight, a commander, a hero" and to convert his victims into mere pixels; Breivik's prideful claim to be a Knight Templar and the dubbing of himself as Justiciar Andrew Berwick in his manifesto were nothing more than realizations of Justicar Andersnordic, Breivik's *Warcraft* handle. Shutting down all discourse about Breivik's politics—"his political ideas explain nothing"—Knausgaard refuses to see Breivik as anything other than a freak aberration from the otherwise civilized and humane culture of Norway. A culture of violent warfare and hatred, derived from video games and contained in solitary confinement with Breivik in prison, extends no further than the limits of his mind.

This is a mistake. It is a mistake to see Breivik's ideas as a total aberration from European politics, and it is a mistake to dismiss Breivik's medievalism out of hand. His medievalism reveals crucial aspects of his motivations, and it also points to the vital importance that the Middle Ages play for so many extremists, especially white suprem-acists and white nationalists, today. A distinction between white nationalism and white supremacy should be made, as they are coterminous but not necessarily interchange-able. Put simply, white supremacy is the belief that a white race is naturally and inherently superior to all other races, and white nationalism is the belief that whites must main-tain cultural, political, and economic hegemony over other groups. It is entirely reasonable to see white nationalism as crypto-white supremacy, wherein a nation is defined primarily by a dominant homogenous culture and lan-guage that is worthier than others. Suddenly, during and after the American and French presidential elections in 2016 and 2017, the general election in the Netherlands, and the federal elections in Germany, it seems as if dis-course about white identity, white supremacy, and white nationalism are everywhere. White identity politics have gone mainstream. In 2011, Breivik's attacks were met with baffled astonishment. Today, they seem increasingly like the most violent recent expression of white resentment, white fear, and white hate.

A youth movement, rejecting multiculturalism and celebrating its own ethnocultural inheritance, has defined itself as Generation Identity. *Generation Identity: A Dec-laration of War Against the '68ers* (2013) is a manifesto by radical right Austrian activist Markus Willinger. In short polemical chapters, the manifesto blasts the baby -boomer generation (whom Willinger calls '68ers) for hav-ing betrayed the indigenous peoples of Europe by destroy-ing their identities via liberal immigration policies and by succumbing to globalism and consumerism. True Euro-pean identities have been forgotten, as "the enemies of all identities"—the multiculturalist enablers—"knowingly destroyed everything that was holy to us and to our ancestors."[24] Generation Identity is a part of growing identitarian movements in Europe and the US championing a white nationalism that proudly celebrates a shared white European heritage. The identitarian movement memorializes and celebrates the European Middle Ages in particular as a time of white cultural unity.

In opposition to refugees and Muslim immigrants, they fly flags that bear the number 732, commemorating the victory over Islamic forces of the Frankish king Charles Martel in the year 732 at the Battle of Tours. Geert Wilders, the Islamophobic Dutch politician and founder of the populist right Parti voor de Vrijheid (Party for Freedom, PVV) in the Netherlands, has praised Hitler for understanding the true violence and bestial nature of Islam, a "cult of hatred" hell-bent since the eighth century on destroying Western civilization.[25] Had Charles Martel and the Franks lost, the West would still today be a poor and uncivilized Islamic colony, in Wilders's view. As in the eighth century, Western civilization must today defend itself against the cult of hatred. Breivik, too, lauds the heroic exploits of the Frankish forces of Charles Martel, and there have been multiple extreme-right groups that have called themselves the Charles Martel Group or the Charles Martel Society, including one anti-Algerian terrorist cell in France in the 1970s and 1980s that was responsible for multiple bombings, killing and wounding two dozen people. Taking their lead from centuries of historians (including Gibbon) who have painted Charles Martel as a saviour of civilization as we know it for his defeat of Islamic forces at Tours, Breivik and other extremists point to the Francian victory over invading Islamic armies for an example of and inspiration for what a unified Europe is capable of, if only Europeans would recognize their common identity.

Breivik's manifesto, reflecting a prevalent and growing identitarian movement on the far and extreme right, is replete with the imprints of a white-nationalist ideology that rejects the viability of modern multicultural society and celebrates the perceived ethnic homogeneity of the Middle Ages. His global Knights Templar network, though obviously fabricated (being explicitly referred to as "a hypothetical fiction group" written "in character" in the manifesto),[26] nevertheless reveals how the concept of a unified medieval resistance against outsiders serves as a template for modern "resistance" movements against so-called Islam and their so-called cultural Marxist enablers.

Medieval European society is seen by some on the far and extreme right today as racialist, in that it acknowledged, embraced, and celebrated its population as a dominant white Christian race. The contemporary fight to proclaim a distinct white European identity is perceived to be an extension and continuation of the medieval order. This is not a wholly novel argument. The American extremist Francis Parker Yockey, whose anti-Semitic polemics supporting fascism in the mid-twentieth century are still influential among white-nationalist circles, wrote of medieval Europe being characterized by its cultural unity: "one race, one nation, and one people" is how Yockey describes Europe in the Middle Ages.[27] Chivalry was an ethical code that shaped common behavioural standards, Latin was a universal language, Christianity was dominant, Roman law was universal, and the Gothic was a unifying aesthetic. The cultural unity of the medieval West, despite national differences, acted as a bulwark against all outside influences and forces. The revolutions of the eighteenth century, spearheaded by anti-Culture Jews (Yockey's term), swept away "our Gothic youth," bringing in its tide individualist materialism and destroying the "monolithic Culture-State-Nation-Race-People" of Europe in the Middle Ages.

White nationalists who call for a white ethnostate look to Yockey as a luminary of their cause. The website of Counter-Currents Publishing, which publishes neo-Nazi and other extremist material, contains blog posts and commenters touting knightly orders like the Knights Hospitallers as defenders of a pan-European imperium of a single medieval Western Christian culture. Militant knights are cast as defenders of European racial identity and culture. Greg Johnson, the editor-in-chief of Counter-Currents, writes, "If you go back far enough in history, you find times, such as the High Middle Ages, when there was a sense of the unity of the European race. Petty state nationalism is a far more modern phenomenon."[28] Modern whiteness and the fight for white identity attempt to recapture the "essential genetic unity" of the white race, a racial unity that the High Middle Ages recognized and protected. Medieval Christendom was essentially racialist at its core.

Fascists place the medieval at the core of their ideology by fashioning the period as originary and embryonic. The website of the English Defence League (EDL), the most conspicuous extreme-right street movement in the UK since the fascist National Front in the 1970s, explicitly resists leftists who disavow an English identity that was forged in the Middle Ages. Two so-called "common" beliefs are discarded by the EDL: first, that Englishness and English culture started in the Victorian period; second, that there is no distinctly English culture, a belief that is ascribed to revolutionary young Marxists. The EDL then lists the "foundations" of Englishness that were established "in Anglo-Saxon times and have been built upon ever since," including the concept of individual freedom, the values of Magna Carta, critical thinking, nursery rhymes, Christian heritage, and "our civil society."[29] Englishness has a long heritage and "a serious, civilisation-forming, world-changing core." Characterized by a commitment to racial and national communitarianism, the EDL and others on the extreme right insist that our identities are grounded in shared cultural traditions. Beyond the EDL and the UK, populist right parties across Europe, especially but not exclusively in France, Austria, Greece, Germany, and the Netherlands, have challenged and contrasted libertarian-universalistic values with traditionalist-communitarian values as such parties have turned to identity politics. Multiculturalism is accused of destroying traditional norms and in turn the organic national (racial) community.

The call to return to ancestral and spiritual values is a hallmark of extreme-right politics. A term—archeofuturism—has been coined by French nationalist Guillaume Faye to describe a return to ancestral values via a coming together of traditionalism and futurism. Archeofuturism holds that the progressive philosophies of egalitarianism and progress are dying, and that the future requires "an archaic mind-set": a pre-modern and non-humanistic outlook, returning to the "ancestral values" that underlie the social order.[30] "Our folk"—by which Faye implies the various peoples of Europe, whether French, Italian, Czech, or Russians, and so on—must embrace "ancestral virility" (21). He invokes Nietzsche as his primary inspiration for revolution and rebirth, a common move for the extreme right; a Tumblr page for Radical Traditionalism, for example, quotes Nietzsche on its banner: "We know that the man of the future will be the man with the longest memory."[31] The transcendent values of ancestral European life have been devastated by modern life, and those who properly remember the timeless spiritual values of pre-modernity gain insight into a cultural life that only they can see. For Faye, leftist multiculturalists are unable and obstinately unwilling to see the spiritual life of true Europeans. He names them "ethnomasochists," self-hating people who feel shame at their home culture and ethnicity and strive to destroy Europe's authentic ancestral culture. "[O]ur memory and our blood" are being erased and drained by such ethnomasochists. Archeofuturism speaks to the intertwined relationship between past and future. Identity only has meaning and force insofar as it is a continuous thread.

Observing and hoping for the continued dissipation of the power of European nation-states, Faye calls for a new "authentic imperialism" that would be very different from the European Union, a failed experiment that will continue to promote political chaos by imagining Europe to be unified by common rights rather than by culture and identity. Faye is all for European unity but opposed to the European Union. He instead imagines a contemporary unified Europe as a "neo-Carolingian community" and advocates a European as opposed to a French or German or Belgian nationalism.[32] Seeing Europe as a racial federation comprised of his fellow European compatriots like Catalans, Lombards, and Antwerpians, all non-Europeans—Africans, Arabs, Chinese, and so on—are not and can never be truly European. Once unified by the archaic and ancestral values of the Roman Empire and by medieval Christendom, Europe has declined since the eighteenth century, when equality and individualism came to be prioritized over communal, national, and ethnic consciousness. But the lost unity of Rome and medieval Europe is being remembered and reconstructed today as identitarianism takes hold among the "awoken."

Echoing the thought of Yockey, many on the far and extreme right consider pan-Europeanism and cultural, political, and ethnic imperium to be the legacy of medieval Europe. To some of the more intellectually inclined of the racist white-nationalists, the very notions of the political right and left represent a split not only between traditionalism and individualism, but between the medieval and the modern. Michael O'Meara, a white-nationalist writer who translates extreme-right material into English and calls for the establishment of a white ethnostate, locates the origins of the divergence between the notions of the political right and left in the late Middle Ages, when European society was de-feudalized by the urban merchant class, an "anti-traditional concentration of power" that upended "aristocratic prerogative and ecclesiastical authority."[33] The right, bolstered by the conservative forces of language, custom, and regional identity, emerged as a reaction to these bourgeois subversions of the feudal state. In such an account it is possible to see Europe's entire political history since the Middle Ages as "the story of the right's progressive decline" (11). The right defends the traditions and communal identity born in the medieval period, while the left disempowers and destroys these ancestral communities by denying the very existence of European ethnic identity.

Ancient and medieval Europeans, in O'Meara's thought, understood that a person's freedoms do not derive from one's humanity, but from one's participation in a social and political community. Following Descartes, Enlightenment liberalism made the unencumbered individual into a totally free agent that formed society's basic component. The modern individual became divorced from social communities and became conceived as a world unto himself. Ancient democracy was founded on communal, not human, rights; one was afforded political rights because one was a member of a community, not because one was human. As opposed to liberalism's concept of the individual as detached from society, "ancient and medieval notions of freedom held that one was free to the degree one was able to participate in the community" (246), according to O'Meara. With the loss of the concept of the necessity of the social community came the loss of an organic notion of a single people, defined, essentially, by their culture. The group is central; the individual must feel that they belong to a cultural family.

This is, of course, a way of arguing for a white ethnostate. There are our traditions and our history and there are your traditions and your history. Medieval states are cast as white states. As with Yockey, for O'Meara chivalry, knighthood, universities, and Gothic cathedrals were authentic expressions of a core European spirit that emanated from Celtic-Germanic paganism. Medieval and early modern Christianity are praised for adapting to this core ancestral spirit and having in turn prohibited miscegenation and accepted the reality of racial difference. "The ancient, medieval, and epic traditions of European thought" are in many ways "superior" (269) to modern progressive beliefs, primarily for having recognized and accepted the whiteness of Europeanness.

The dream of a white homeland with foundations in medieval Europe thrives among racist white-nationalists. Culture is depicted as a thing that only gains distinction and legitimacy over many centuries. Bede and Beowulf are given key roles in forming a national psyche and identity and traditional values. Proclaiming the degradation of true—white—Englishness today, the openly white-supremacist writer David Abbott proudly describes the coming of the Anglo-Saxons to Britain: "Englishness goes back a long way," he assures us, pointing to Alfred describing the English people (the "Angelcynn") and the fact that the language was called English, not Saxon, as an indication that the English were a race, despite the fact that we have no clear idea why it was called English and not Saxon.[34] (Most likely it is because they were the English Saxons, as opposed to the Old Saxons of Germany). Abbott's point is to establish the right to call the English "indigenous": "Surely a race that has lived in a land for fifteen hundred years, with that land being named after them, has the right to be called indigenous" (38). He cares about this right, of course, as a means to argue that the island belongs to the English and that people who do not trace their identity to the English Middle Ages are outsiders; that there is an essence to the "native" English and that others cannot adapt to this essence.

Race exists; indeed, an English race, consisting of the bloodstock of Danes, Normans, and Saxons, exists. The medieval invasions by the Vikings and Normans, described in vivid detail in Abbott's account, apparently did not really affect true Englishness in any meaningful way. Those medieval invasions were productive invasions, fusing blood kin, unlike the new invasions of the non-white. Abbott imagines the thousand-year anniversary of the Norman Conquest as being marked by William the Conquered and the Grand Mullah of England, rather than an archbishop, greeting the new Muslim prime minister. The English race—white English citizens—are called on to defend their "birthright," which was established in the Middle Ages.

The necessary-defence argument is boilerplate for the extreme right. This argument holds that "ethnic" Europeans must recognize themselves as a distinct cultural unit, as was properly recognized in the Middle Ages, and defend that culture against outsiders, as was properly done in the Middle Ages. Troy Southgate, a neo-Nazi and advocate for the English New Right (and self-avowed National Anarchist), proclaims Alfred the Great's intellectual, political, and martial achievements, admiring the tenth-century king not only for uniting England and the English and defeating the invading Vikings, but as importantly, for recognizing that an enemy without respect for one's culture must be defeated for one's social and cultural needs to flourish.[35] For Southgate, Alfred well understood the relationship between "constructive action" and an intellectual and cultural tradition. In order for the spirit of England and the English people to flourish, barbarian foreigners needed to be eliminated. Southgate sees in Alfred a model predecessor for the sort of political acumen and leadership that we need today—someone who can recognize the necessity to defeat an enemy while also celebrating and advancing his own culture's achievements. Because of Alfred's military successes defending England against outsiders, he was able to then turn his attention to social needs like education. Once the borders are secured, true culture may flourish.

The racist, anti-immigrant, white-nationalist matrix from which Breivik emerged continues to grow and gain political influence. In the next chapter, we will see how American traditionalist conservatives have long aligned US history with Europe's ancient and medieval history, implying a racial connection between the dominant heritages of the two continents. The American extreme right, revitalized as a youth movement akin to Markus Willinger's Generation Identity, explicitly aligns white American Christian ethnic history and culture with Europe's white ethnic history and culture. The most prominent of these American-centred groups of late has been the euphemistically named alt-right, a ragtag collection of racists, fascists, neo-Nazis, hucksters, and trolls whose actions typically do not extend far beyond anonymous posts on websites like Reddit and 4chan. The so-called alt-right is little more than a flashy rebranding of white nationalism and white supremacy. It revels in the tribalism of white golden ages and insists on the need to defend Western (white) civilization and the "traditions" of whiteness. The alt-right movement gained widespread attention during the course of Donald Trump's presidential campaign, which they vociferously supported. Trump's "Make America Great Again" slogan echoes not only the nostalgia but the desire for a white America common amongst white extremists. Richard Spencer, the identitarian de facto leader of the alt-right, rails against multiculturalism, tolerance, and diversity because a country "can't have many peoples in one nation" as one people will naturally dominate the other.[36] Greatness and whiteness are one and the same thing.

Identity is everything for the alt-right. This is neo-Nazism rebranded, in which every individual has an innate sense of the racial and national collectives to which they belong. These collectives define the essence of every person, whatever outer appearances might look like. As Jeffrey Tucker writes of the alt-right, "What appears to be [social] progress is actually loss: loss of culture, identity, and mission. They look back to what they imagine to be a golden age when elites ruled and peons obeyed."[37] At the core of contemporary society is an intrinsic struggle between genders, races, nations, and other collective sources of identity, and the alt-right looks back wistfully on premodernity, when people knew their places and an authoritarian order ruled. The alt-right pitches the Crusades as necessary white fight. They explicitly call for a new Crusade and for all identitarians to embrace a crusader ideal of white struggle against an ever-encroaching multiculturalism that denies and denigrates European—white—identity.[38]

Young American fascists align themselves politically and culturally with the notion of a white Europe. Identity Europa, a California-based white-nationalist group, touts itself on its website as being "a generation of awakened Europeans who have discovered that we are part of the great peoples, history, and civilization that flowed from the European continent. We reject the idea that our identities are mere abstractions to be deconstructed. We oppose those who would defame our history and rich cultural heritage. In a time when every other people are [sic] asserting their identity, without action, we will have no chance to resist our dispossession."[39] Identity Europa claims that every culture and every people has a right to celebrate its heritage and be recognized as a distinct cultural group in order to proclaim that whiteness is itself a distinct, real cultural unit. In turn, because "white European" is as much a valid ethnicity as any other ethnicity, that group has the right to its own homeland and the right to celebrate its culture without shame. Opposition is key to the proclamation of white identity: *they say* white culture is not real, *they say* white culture is not a thing; *we say* look at our heritage. White identity is European identity. *Our* ancestors, *our* history. Identity Europa's posters, echoing Donald Trump's presidential slogan, tout phrases like "Let's become great again" and "Our destiny is ours" and "Protect your heritage" with images of classical sculptures in the background.

The next chapter will examine the medievalizing drive at the heart of American traditional conservatism, but the mission to recapture and redefine America's roots in medieval Europe has seeped into less mainstream venues. The League of the South, which the Southern Poverty Law Center calls a white supremacist, secessionist, neo-Confederate hate group, draws explicit ancestry lines between the traditions of Britain and the South. Southern identity is characterized by the League of the South as being medieval at its core. Their website proclaims, "We trace our ancestors and their deeds because that is who we are. That is our Identity ... Just because we live in what is called the 'modern' world does not mean that the forces of history have been rendered inoperable."[40] This rhetoric is used to warn white readers to resist the "Reconquista" being undertaken by Hispanics, deploying the terminology of the Spanish Christian wars to reclaim territory from Muslim rulers on the Iberian peninsula from the eighth to fifteenth centuries. The League of the South calls for the "South [to return] to its European roots." They learn from medieval combat techniques and persistently refer to their medieval ancestors' insurrections against tyranny as inspiration for modern rebellion. Like the so-called knights of the Ku Klux Klan, the League of the South claims deep roots in the medieval soil of Western Europe. A racist group like the League of the South draws an explicit line between the traditions of Western Europe and the American South, claiming to thrive "in a long community of blood." The League of the South openly calls for a new Confederacy that celebrates the "culture and folk customs" of an organic people that have "one foot in Europe and the other in Dixie." They reject liberal democracy and place the right remembrance of the past at the core of their political agenda.

The League of the South and O'Meara are far from alone in their desire for a reclamation of the authentic, traditional values of an ethnically homogenous people whose political legitimacy is rooted in the longevity of their shared history. Neo-Nazi organizations like the Traditionalist Workers Party, based in the US, use the aesthetics of national socialism in their propaganda to tout their having "100% European Identity, 0% White Guilt"— so says a sticker design that can be downloaded from their website. Even as the far and extreme right in the US and Europe proclaim whiteness as a valid racial identity, they turn to culture, rather than skin colour, as the clearest evidence of the existence of a disparate white race. For many on the far right, whether they call themselves the alt-right or identitarians or something else, identity is lauded and paraded above all. Even if extremist websites and podcasts are nearly explicit references to Nazism— the Daily Stormer, the Daily Shoah (a crass pun on the *Daily Show*)—they rarely openly proclaim Nazism. Instead, they are identitarians. It is their European heritage that gives their lives and identities shape and meaning and separates them from others whose "roots" are planted outside of Europe.

Notes

[24] Markus Willinger, *Generation Identity: A Declaration of War Against the '68ers*, trans. David Schreiber (London: Arktos, 2013), p. 102.

[25] Wilders points to Hitler's wish that the Franks had lost in 732 so that Europe could have been converted to the violence and heroism extolled by the Islamic religion. See *Marked for Death: Islam's War Against the West and Me* (Washington, DC: Regnery, 2012), p. 42.

[26] Anders Behring Breivik, "2083: A European Declaration of Independence," *public intelligence*, July 28, 2011, https://publicintelligence.net/anders-behring-breiviks-complete-manifesto-2083-a-european-declaration-of-independence/ (accessed January 15, 2017).

[27] Francis Parker Yockey, "The Proclamation of London," https://archive.org/details/TheProclamationOfLondon (accessed November 18, 2016).

[28] Greg Johnson, "Explicit White Nationalism," *Counter Currents*, October 4, 2010, http://www.counter-currents.com/2010/10/explicit-white-nationalism/ (accessed November 13, 2016).

[29] http://www.englishdefenceleague.org.uk/we-are-proud-of-english-culture/ (accessed December 20, 2016).

[30] Guillaume Faye, *Archeofuturism: European Visions of the Post-Catastrophic Age* (London: Arktos, 2010), pp. 13–14.

[31] http://radical-traditionalism.tumblr.com (accessed January 13, 2017).

[32] Guillaume Faye, *Why we Fight: Manifesto of the European Resistance*, trans. Michael O'Meara (London: Arktos, 2011), p. 50.

[33] Michael O'Meara, *New Culture, New Right: Anti-Liberalism in Postmodern Europe* (London: Arktos, 2013), p. 11.

[34] David Abbott, *Dark Albion: A Requiem for the English* (Ramsgate: Sparrow, 2012), p. 7.

[35] Troy Southgate, *Tradition and Revolution: Collected Writings of Troy Southgate* (London: Arktos, 2010), p. 31.

[36] Richard Spencer, Twitter Post, December 29, 2016, 12:01 p.m., https://twitter.com/RichardBSpencer/status/814516635247575040 (accessed January 29, 2017).

[37] Jeffrey Tucker, "Five Differences between the Alt-Right and Libertarianism," *Foundation for Economic Education*, August 26, 2016, https://fee.org/articles/five-differences-between-the-alt-right-and-libertarians/ (accessed September 20, 2016).

[38] Gregory Hood, "The Great Crusade," *Radix Journal*, February

24, 2015, http://www.radixjournal.com/journal/2015/2/24/the-great
-crusade (accessed November 11, 2016).

[39] https://www.identityevropa.com (accessed January 5, 2017).

[40] http://leagueofthesouth.com/in-defense-of-our-blood/ (accessed
May 25, 2016).

Chapter 3

Inheritance, Roots, Traditions: Discovering Medieval Origins

Edmund Burke and Traditionalist Conservatism

Despite the fanaticism of Breivik, Guillaume Faye, or the League of the South, some of the extreme right's formative ideas about heritage and tradition emanate from more mainstream right-wing discourse. The extremists make explicit what is at times implied by mainstream traditionalist conservative discourse concerning the triumph and superiority of white European culture. To both, the Middle Ages often serve as the bedrock of an "authentic" cultural heritage. In certain strands of European and American political discourse there is a search and a desire for historically grounded, organic traditions that embody the core of a national and cultural spirit. It is in this sense that the medieval plays a key role in the politics of the right today. Yet political medievalism is not a solely contemporary phenomenon. The Middle Ages have been central to the imaginations of conservative thought in Europe since the late eighteenth century.

So entrenched is the notion of tradition to conservatives that it can serve as a shorthand for conservatism itself; the term "conservatism" implies a conservation of things past. In lamenting the progressivism of academia,

Roger Scruton starts his right-wing instructional manual, *How to Be a Conservative*, by juxtaposing the materialist, socialist left with "traditional values" or "any claim that might be made for the high achievements of Western civilization."[41] Conservatives take comfort in enjoying a "settled and affirmative culture," by which Scruton appears to mean a non-contested and sacred space where grand narratives of triumph are considered holy truths. We must be proud of that culture and history: Greek and Roman, Judaism and Christianity, and medieval epics and romances make us who we are: "they are *ours* ... they form part of what made us, and convey the message that it is right to be who we are" (91). For Scruton, Western culture needs no justification or qualification. It must be championed.

Some on the hard right see modernity as a betrayal of tradition. For Enlightenment thinkers, the traditional was equivalent with dogmatic ignorance, yet "tradition" and the "traditional" today can stand in as euphemisms for nativism, nationalism, and chauvinism. The notion of tradition is, of course, at the very core of conservatism. Promoting and defending the traditions of a culture or nation or people is a crucial part of the conservative agenda, whether we are discussing the conservatism of Edmund Burke in the late eighteenth century or a conservative politician today. The manner in which "tradition" is framed, though, speaks volumes about how far right a conservative really is. Although cheers for tradition could by default or insinuation include the Middle Ages, conservatives of different stripes have been explicit about seeing the medieval as both foundation and model. Traditionalist conservatism, sometimes referred to as classical conservatism or Burkean conservatism, rejects egalitarianism, liberalism, individualism, and utilitarianism, and vaunts communal, organic unity, heritage, and cultural traditions as the foundations of civil society.[42]

Traditionalist conservatism is by no means a recent phenomenon, with a genealogy stretching back to the late eighteenth century. The man generally considered to be the founding father of conservatism is Edmund Burke, at least in the English-speaking world. To some in his own day he was a shrewd visionary; to others, a quixotic madman who confused romance with reality. Burke held tradition in the highest of esteem. In his famous treatise declaring and justifying his opposition to the early days of the French Revolution, *Reflections on the Revolution in France* (1790), Burke contends that all necessary reforms undertaken by Britain, from Magna Carta to the Glorious Revolution of 1688, were enacted within the framework of the unique, organic traditions of Britain and the British people. The rights and liberties afforded to British subjects are founded upon their inheritance from past centuries. "People will not look forward to posterity," Burke declares, "who never look backward to their ancestors."[43] Civil institutions only garner legitimacy and reverence through age; for Burke, the past legitimizes the present. There is indeed a social contract, but it is much more than a flimsy business deal. It is "a partnership not only between those who are living, but between those who are living, those who are dead, and those who are to be born" (96). Burke holds the idea of a hierarchical order gluing society together as an indisputable truth.

Primarily because these terms had not yet replaced "Gothick" or the "Dark Ages," the words "medieval" and "Middle Ages" do not appear in Burke's *Reflections*; nevertheless, the book is tinged with reverence for and awe of the medieval period. Burke's perception of the cultural and political traditions of Britain was medieval in nature. Burke went further than espousing general thoughts about nameless ancestors and vague traditions. These venerable things were distinctly medieval. The British of the late eighteenth century were not different from their forebears of centuries past, and Burke breathes a sigh of relief that the British had not "lost the generosity and dignity of thinking of the fourteenth century" (86). The moral and governmental principles of the Middle Ages still undergird and inform the constitution of Britain centuries later. He grieves for the death and deep burial of the age of chivalry and the glory of Europe, the replacing of "manly sentiment and heroic enterprize" (76) by workaday bureaucrats and pencil pushers. In the age of chivalry, the fundamental principles of fealty and manners tempered the tyranny of kings and lent an ennobling equality to the whole of the social order. It was perhaps no accident that Thomas Paine and others called him Don Quixote; in his writing we can see Burke passionately trying to preserve something of a period long gone, doing so in a romantic and perhaps partially blinded way.

Burke laid the groundwork for the adulation of the Middle Ages that would become a hallmark of traditionalist conservatism from the nineteenth century through today. What appeals to the traditionalist conservative about the Middle Ages is an image of the period's holistic community, the notion that there existed then an organic unity across social classes, and that values like honour, nobility, and loyalty prevailed. For the traditionalist conservative, the modern world is a world of loss: the loss of communal identity, of an organic society, of timeless and universal truths and values. The medieval in turn acts as a premodern model of solidarity and order. Burke thus idealizes the Middle Ages as an age of faith, stability, and harmonious social relations, where communal ties were respected and moored every individual to family, clan, town, and nation.[44]

The American Conservative Medieval

Although traditionalism as a political school of thought in the West dates to Burke's defence of the transcendent values of religion, family, and the state, modern traditionalist conservatism is really an American phenomenon, at least in its beginnings. American conservative intellectuals after the Second World War were heavily influenced by eighteenth- and nineteenth-century English traditionalists and anti-Enlightenment thinkers like Carlyle, Arnold, and Disraeli. The ideal of upholding what appears to be traditional is at the heart of conservatism, so even if political discourse regularly dabbles in dark medievalism, the right wing of the political spectrum maintains and promotes the necessity of defending traditions, which often will have medieval roots. This is not a solely European phenomenon. Although American politicians will regularly invoke dark medievalism, as discussed in the first chapter, a certain branch of American conservatives draws a connection between Western European culture and history and that of the United States to enshrine particular narratives of a common identity.

The medieval has been a cornerstone of traditionalist conservatism in the US from its postwar rise. As conservatism became a viable intellectual and political school of thought in the US after the Second World War, a number of American traditionalist conservatives went digging for and unearthed America's medieval roots. Their aim, in short, has been to solidify America's roots deeper in the past than the founding of Jamestown, and beyond solely ancient, pagan Greece. These postwar American conservatives especially admired medieval Christianity, longing for a God-centred world filled with genuine piety, but also admiring chivalric manners and a society in which honour and virtue reigned supreme. Postwar American traditionalist conservatives averted their gaze from the horrors of totalitarianism and genocide, and discovered in the medieval past an age of tranquillity and discipline. They saw the United States as a beacon and fortress of transcendent values and moral order, set against the secularism and moral relativism of the Soviet Union and China.

Finishing his doctoral thesis in 1943, Richard Weaver was a prominent force driving American traditionalist conservatism in the postwar period. As a faculty member at the University of Chicago, Weaver dreamed of his native South, writing a series of essays and books on Southern chivalry, Southern agrarianism, and the traditional values of the Old South, which he saw as a counterbalance to totalitarianism. Weaver defended Southern feudalism because it "possessed stability" and "was a rooted culture which viewed with dismay the anonymity and social indifference of urban man."[45] The juxtaposition of an alienating, calculating, officious, bureaucratic, and technocratic North, as opposed to the God-centred world where chivalric manners reigned, was key to the thought of Weaver and other postwar traditionalist conservatives. It was the belief of Frederick Wilhelmsen, a mid-late twentieth-century neo-Thomist philosopher, that "conservatives have lost our kings and our chivalry; our craftsmen are gone, and our peasantry is fast disappearing." For Wilhelmsen, as for Weaver, what the Middle Ages offered that modernity does not was a Christian culture where each individual had a place—and knew it.

Weaver's most well-known work, *Ideas Have Consequences* (1948), was inspired by the ideal of chivalry, according to Weaver himself.[46] Modern life had produced the carnage of the twentieth century and would produce more if unchecked. For Weaver, the ideal of chivalry worked as a restraining spiritual force that checked and contained the brutality of warfare and violence. Chivalry insisted that war could be controlled, though Weaver admits, in a rather massive understatement, that "there were episodes in the age of chivalry which make unpleasant reading" (30). But, nevertheless, chivalry was the kind of "moderating influence" that modern warfare does not have, which strives for total victory at all costs, with no regard for civilian lives or the rights of the enemy. The defenceless labourers and inhabitants of the fields and villages burned and pillaged in *chevauchées*—wide-scale, deliberate, calculated raids meant to destroy enemy territory and undermine the legitimacy of the enemy's government—during the Hundred Years' War might, perhaps, like to have a few words with Weaver on chivalry.

Weaver's conservatism, by his account, grew from his feelings of despair during the Second World War. In response to global chaos, Weaver began to believe that the world "will not regain order and stability until it returns to the kind of poetic-religious vision which dominated the Middle Ages."[47] He concludes *Ideas Have Consequences* by hoping for a "passionate reaction, like that which flowered in the chivalry and spirituality of the Middle Ages" against "the waning day of the West" (168). Weaver did not simply retreat from the modern world by gazing back at an orderly and peaceful medieval past; he called for the South to lead the United States back to the future, forging a society of honour and right. The notion of Southern chivalry was much more than superficial gentlemanliness. For Weaver, Southern chivalry was actually a direct descendant of the genuine chivalric tradition of the Middle Ages. That tradition arose in order to counteract the savage cruelty of European society after the death of Charlemagne, in the same way that the modern world needed a counterbalance against its own barbarities. Weaver has some difficulty explaining how a medieval code of conduct made its way to the American South, but is certain nonetheless that it came in the form of a seed and soon sprouted into the Southern gentleman caste. Tison Pugh has shown how white Southern masculinity has long celebrated itself as chivalry reborn,[48] but Weaver's Southern chivalry was no rebirth: it was a direct descendant. Chivalry of the American South is the Middle Ages's true heir and perhaps last gasp. Certain strands of Weaver's thought are strikingly similar to the extremist, white supremacist League of the South.

The group that Weaver was associated with were known as the New Conservatives, whose ideas gave shape and form to modern American conservatism. An enduring and towering figure for the American right, Russell Kirk is generally considered to be perhaps the most important New Conservative who played a crucial role in giving postwar traditionalist conservatism an intellectual shape. His 1953 work, *The Conservative Mind*, is a cornerstone of twentieth-century American conservatism and is still widely studied as a foundational book of the conservative movement. By offering a primer of conservative thought from Burke to T. S. Eliot, the *Conservative Mind* helped to situate conservatism as a legitimate political philosophy. Kirk considered his thought to be a continuation of Burke, and, as with Burke, the Middle Ages are key to Kirk's historical frameworks. Late in life, in the 1990s, Kirk echoed M. Stanton Evans's warnings about the cultural anarchy produced by multiculturalists, arguing that only a renewed love of "an inherited culture" and a recognition that the American social order "is part of a great continuity and essence" can save America from moral and cultural decay.[49] The core of American culture was inherited from Britain, and Kirk impresses the vital importance of transfixing an intelligent high culture, of which the Middle Ages are a key part. This higher American culture began with the Anglo-Saxons, though it really progressed with the Normans and their "French imagination" that awoke the

"English mind" so that the post-Conquest English peasantry, who did not care much for proper grammar, crafted
a flexible language capable of literary poetry and prose.

Kirk went looking for the roots of American culture and
what he called "American order," by which Kirk means the
social and moral character holding together the spirit of
the nation and people. In the Middle Ages, Kirk found a
"neglected inheritance": "Knowledge of medieval England
and Scotland is essential to a decent understanding of
American order." In the Middle Ages, Kirk argues, the systems of governance and law that the US inherited arose;
the language that Americans speak and the literature that
they read developed; industry and commerce that are
fundamental to modern economies evolved; architecture
and universities developed; and, amusingly, also "the idea
of a gentleman that still may be discerned in the American democracy."[50] That America's founding figures did not
effusively praise the Middle Ages is for Kirk no impedi-
ment to his belief that the period was seen as fundamental to them—just the opposite. Their medieval inheritance
was so taken for granted that they did not even bother
talking about it. But Kirk finds that the vital inheritance
has over time been denigrated and forgotten, and sets
out to right wrongs.

Traditionalist conservatism in the vein of Burke, Weaver,
and Kirk is not quite the philosophy of some of the American right in the twenty-first century, especially of the market conservatives who decry the intrusion of government
into the private sector and champion free and unfettered
markets. But the stress placed on "family values" by the
Republican Party does echo some traditionalist rhetoric
about moral order and timeless values, and a large per-
centage of the American right today are evangelical social
conservatives. Having catalyzed and given shape to the
contemporary right in the US, much of which continues to

press the need for the traditional values of a pious Christian society, the legacy of the New Conservatives lives on. Many contemporary American conservatives, not surprisingly, valorize the American rather than the European past. But digging past execrable bullet points about medieval torture, today we can find sectors of the American right in both the mainstream and beyond touting America's medieval roots and the traditional values handed down to the nation from medieval Europe, especially medieval Britain.

Consider the sociologist Rodney Stark, for example. Stark writes popular triumphalist histories of Christianity and the West with titles such as *The Victory of Reason: How Christianity Led to Freedom, Capitalism, and Western Success* (2005), *God's Battalions: The Case for the Crusades* (2009), and *The Triumph of Christianity* (2011). In a recent work, *How the West Won: The Neglected Story of the Triumph of Modernity* (2014), Stark, in a move characteristic for the right, calls his book "unfashionable" because it acts as a corrective to the politically correct lies of multiculturalists who denigrate Western civilization.[51] He characterizes himself as a rectifier of misguided left-wing scholarship. A crucial part of Stark's counter-history is the saving of the Middle Ages from its detractors; he calls the period between 500 and 1200 "The Not-so-Dark Ages" (66). Stark positions modernity and the West—interchangeable terms for him—as a combination of the cultural and political values of Greece and the spiritual values of medieval Christianity. His revisionist history—this is how he implicitly and at times explicitly characterizes it—sees the fall of Rome not as destructive but as supremely beneficial for the rise of Western civilization, because it led to the disintegration of large-scale empire that "unleashed creative competition among hundreds of independent political units" (69) which resulted in progress. Progress for Stark is the result of "creative disunity," by which he means that the interne-

cine warfare of medieval Europe led to technological progress. Peace, for Stark, is boring; worse, it is unproductive.
Instead of lauding Charlemagne's reign as a high point
of the early Middle Ages, Stark cheekily calls his rule an
"interlude" because it centralized power and thus stymied
growth. On the disintegration of the Carolingian Empire
under Charlemagne's three sons, Stark exclaims, "Europe's
precious disunity was restored!" (91). Stark traces the rise,
triumph, and superiority of the West to freedom: the freedom to "hope" and to "act" and to "invest." That freedom
"emerged during the so-called Dark Ages. The ramifica-
tions would be felt for centuries to come" (139). Here we
see the recovery and rediscovery of the Middle Ages cast
as an untold, buried, or secret history. The "true" medieval is the bedrock of western progress and freedom, but
progressives have buried that truth in their pursuit of an
all-inclusive multiculturalist narrative of progress. Such
a narrative has come at the expense of the "real" West.

Traditionalist conservatism and the legacy of Burke in
America lives on in journals like *The American Conservative* (co-founded by Pat Buchanan) and on websites like
Front Porch Republic and *The Russell Kirk Center for Cultural Renewal*, where high-minded conservatives tend
to see themselves as espousing a principled, reformist,
authentic conservatism. Rod Dreher, a traditionalist conservative writer and blogger and self-proclaimed "crunchy
con," a sort of ecologically minded conservative movement catalyzed by Dreher, sees himself as continuing
the work of Russell Kirk by stressing the ancient truths
of traditional values. In a 2006 book laying out the fundamental principles of his crunchy conservatism movement,
Dreher concludes by calling for his adherents to form
"monastic communities" and to become "our own Bene-
dicts," referring to St. Benedict, the sixth-century saint
who helped inspire the rise of Christian monasticism.[52] In

Dreher's account, crunchy cons in the twenty-first century are following the ways of Benedict, who encouraged early medieval urbanites to leave cities and form rural Christian communities. Having tired of the empty materialism of city life, these green conservatives are living closer to the land by buying food from local farmers and raising their children away from popular culture and mass media. They will build monastery walls around themselves and live the contemplative life. Dreher calls his strategy to reconnect with the divine and live a medieval-like contemplative life the "Benedict option."

Writing for *The American Conservative* in 2015, Dreher calls for a new Middle Age, what he promises will be "a spiritual revolution in a time of spiritual and cultural darkness."[53] Dreher pumps up his readers with a cry of "We can do this!"—meaning resacralizing our lives today and turning inwards in a kind of new Christian renaissance. Dreher writes often of the Middle Ages as a spiritually unified time and of revivifying the medieval bond between individuals and the divinity. He idealizes more than just a spiritual unity of the Middle Ages, writing also of the centrality of tradition to that society, associating traditions with the medieval and solipsistic individualism with the modern. Traditionalist conservatives thus continue to promote their desire to save the Middle Ages from infamy. In the pages of *The American Conservative*, self-described "counter-narratives" hail the medieval as "the nearest man has come to building a Christian society," a society filled with "our medieval ancestors" who "were observant and creative."[54] The "bright, shining lie" of the Enlightenment's narrative of a Dark Ages is reversed: it is the Middle Ages that were enlightened and the modern period that is dark. The Whiggish story of continual progress that dominates the contemporary progressive mindset must be put to rest, and the right must embrace its past. It must look to the traditions of medieval ancestors and rebuild Western civilization in its image.

A key tenet of traditionalist conservatism is that the home culture—nation, continent, the West—is under attack and must be defended against its detractors both at home and abroad. For the far-right American pundit Pat Buchanan (a self-described "paleoconservative"), history is not something of which the West or the US ought to be ashamed. History ought to inspire. Buchanan has long insisted on the patriotic need to laud heroes and celebrate ancestors, warning against Marxists and progressives who seek to demonize white America by defaming their history. The "[u]ltimate goal," Buchanan wrote of "Cultural Marxists" in the 1990s: "Destroy patriotism, kill the love of country, demoralize the people, deconstruct America. History then will no longer unite and inspire us, but depress and divide us into the children of victims and the children of the villains of America's past."[55] Multiculturalists seek to slander and divide the "real" America by destroying its history. More recently, Buchanan continues to rail against an educational system that discriminates against white culture, and he celebrates Donald Trump as the "Great White Hope."[56]

Here is cultural return, rediscovery, and recovery through the eyes of an American white nationalist. Buchanan's distinction between the truth of white history and the falsehoods of multiculturalist history draws common ground between trans-Atlantic cultures. Buchanan has used the rhetoric of a crusade to describe his goals: "Join my crusade for America," he told a cheering crowd when running for President in 1992, a crusade that was being waged to "[take] back our country, [restore] our country to the traditions and ideals upon which it was founded."[57] The rhetoric of "taking back" a nation or making it great again continues to be well-trodden ground well after Buchanan's early 1990s dog whistle, especially for supporters of Donald Trump and equally for Leave supporters in the 2016 Brexit vote. A key ideological component of such rhetoric is a theme that is common among traditionalist conservatives: setting the historical record straight, performing recovery and truth-telling. The right-wing traditionalist's history is true history that recaptures the glory of the nation's past from its detractors: that is, from multiculturalist progressives, especially intellectual and academic leftists (or perceived leftists). Some mainstream commentators will be troublingly explicit about who they are saving history from. M. Stanton Evans, a right-wing journalist (who had the "courage," in a 2007 book, to defend Joseph McCarthy as a misunderstood victim who was actually himself the target of a witch hunt), promised in the mid-1990s to exhume a "cultural record buried out of public view" by the modern educational system. This artefact from the ancient past that lies buried deep in the earth is nothing other than "white, male-dominated, European studies," which had been buried alive by "Afrocentric, feminist, gay, and other counterculture teachings."[58] Multiculturalists, for Evans, don't understand the real America. The real America's roots lay not only in the ancient Greek notion of liberty but in the medieval liberties guaranteed by Magna Carta. Left-wing historians misread and abuse the Middle Ages by castigating it as a time of unblinking and thoughtless piety. *Real* history knows better. For Evans, the Middle Ages "nourished the institutions of free government" (150) and the Renaissance's rejection of medieval liberty led to despotism.

European "Traditions"

When "tradition" or "heritage" are invoked in European political discourse, they often point to a vague and hazy past, whether that of the nation or a culture. On the further reaches of the right, references to the Middle Ages become more specific and more intense. Despite the blurry and obvious nostalgia of past golden ages, calls to preserve tradition and heritage remain politically potent and viable. Even if Eric Hobsbawm showed us over thirty years ago that seemingly age-old traditions are often fairly recent constructions designed to resemble timeworn connections to the past,[59] the appeal of the "traditional" nevertheless remains poignant. The pull of the traditional is, of course, a mainstay of the rhetoric of the full spectrum of the political right.

Picking up the mantle laid down by Burke, traditionalist conservatism became a right-wing rallying cry in the twentieth century, both before and after the Second World War. Today, the European right extols cultural and political traditions emanating from the past, especially the medieval past, as the basis and foundation for political legitimacy. The Statement of Principles of the anti-immigrant, anti-multiculturalist, nationalist Britain First party represents a far-right version of this adulation of heritage. Britain First, formed in 2011 by former members of the British National Party, promises to safeguard the interests of "[g]enuine British citizens" as well as "British history, traditions, culture, and customs."[60] A more mainstream version of traditionalism in British and European politics can be seen in the mission statement of the Cornerstone group, a faction of British Conservative MPs committed to promoting "traditional" British values. They claim to be "dedicated to the traditional values which have shaped the British way of life throughout this country's history";

they purport to "believe in the spiritual values which have informed British institutions, her culture, and her nation's sense of identity for centuries."[61] Both the far-right Britain First and the more mainstream right Cornerstone position themselves against political correctness. It is the "ancient liberties" of Britain, according to the Cornerstone group, that give shape to an authentic British identity.

The far right, though, particularly in northern Europe, is united in part by its opposition to the European Union, as we can see with Marine Le Pen. The EU is charged with sapping and erasing identity and community in lieu of an individualist globalism that dilutes and boils ethnicity, race, and heritage into a single, homogenous pot. In the last few years, a rise in immigration, coupled with a rise in terrorist attacks, especially in northern Europe, has lent a degree of prestige and credibility to far-right populist parties and figures. An "indigenous" people is juxtaposed with and placed in opposition to progressive elites who denigrate that "indigenous" population by welcoming and protecting immigrants and anyone else perceived as an outsider. Nigel Farage, the former leader of the populist United Kingdom Independence Party (UKIP) and an outspoken and prominent supporter of the Leave campaign in the 2016 Brexit vote, construed Brexit as a showdown between the people and political power. Regularly referring to the Leave vote as a political uprising and revolt against the establishment, Farage regarded a vote for Britain to leave the European Union as nativist vengeance: "This is our chance as a people to get back at a political class that has given away everything this nation has ever stood for, everything our forebears ever fought for."[62] It was the "native" people versus the traitorous politicians. "We want our country back," Farage cried. The takeaway from the multifarious and sometimes overwrought analyses in the wake of the 2016 Brexit vote has been what many commentators saw as a Manichean divide between the xenophobic, anti-immigrant Leave camp and the globalist, multiculturalist Remain camp. From the perspective of the far right, this line of commentary has unfairly maligned working-class British voters.

Beyond Brexit and the British Isles, the wider European hard-right positions itself as the defender of European and national traditions, opposed to left-wing progressives (or, depending how far right one is, "cultural Marxists") who are portrayed as cultural relativists desiring the dissolution of all national identities. This is precisely what Marine Le Pen means when she warns of a European Union that "betrays national interests and popular sovereignty and that throws our countries wide open to massive immigration and arrogant finance."[63] The representatives of European far-right political parties are often referred to as "Eurosceptics," but that is something of a misnomer, in that it implies a total opposition to the idea of Europe itself, when it really only applies to their opposition to the European Union. Basking in the glow of the victory of the *Front National* in 2014, Marine Le Pen reflected proudly on "the return of the nation" and the "rediscovered love of our country" to primacy. She lauded the death knell of federalized politics.[64] In the process of rediscovering patriotism and this return to the nation, Le Pen looked forward to the recovery of true French identity. But if Le Pen is a Eurosceptic, such a title can only be applied to her opposition to the European Union. In her speech, she did not reject the idea of Europe: "We must build another Europe, a Europe of free and sovereign nations and freely decided cooperation."[65]

Marine Le Pen promises to safeguard the old while welcoming the new. Return, rediscovery, recovery—of the spirit of France, of the nation, of identity; and on the other hand, a new Europe, one in which each of its sovereign independent nations finds and promotes its traditions and rejects that which is not traditionally national. Her language of rediscovery and recapturing of past glory and tradition forms the heart of traditionalist conservatism, which idealizes the past as a model for the present. It is thus not quite correct to label Le Pen a Eurosceptic. Her position echoes the larger European right: she is sceptical of a European Union that she views as a failed progressive experiment in multiculturalism, but desires to embrace longstanding Western, European, and French identities that are not contradictory but integral to each other. These identities, for Le Pen and the larger European right, are grounded in the medieval past.

Le Pen's stage show is more magisterial than others about the primacy of the medieval in today's world. It is impossible to miss the giant golden statue of Joan of Arc next to which the *Front National* holds its annual May Day rallies in Paris; it is equally impossible to miss the frequent references made by different generations of the Le Pens touting the achievements of Clovis and Charlemagne. Marine Le Pen has written of her desire to recover and rebuild the unity of the nation, a desire that she claims was also felt by the Maid of Orleans. A strong French identity rooted in authentic French traditions is necessary to combat globalism and crass Americanism. Marine Le Pen calls for a reconstruction of French identity grounded in the embrace and celebration of a timeless French spirit. The real Europe consists of proud nation-states celebrating their cultural identities.

The divide between freedom-loving nationalists and cosmopolitan bureaucrats has been a refrain of the European right over the last few years. Geert Wilders speaks acerbically of this divide in his book *Marked for Death* (2012): "Everyday Europeans have been victimized by a cynical, condescending cultural elite that loathe their own people's supposed illiberalism, intolerance, lack of sophistication, and inexplicable attachment to their traditional values. These ruling cosmopolitans do not see European culture as a tradition worth defending, but as a constantly evolving political project. In this utopian scheme, everyday people are reviled for their cultural conservatism, while immigrants are lionized precisely because they are not attached to those traditions" (180). Note the overlap between Wilders's defence of European cultural traditions and Marine Le Pen's. Though they are both on the front lines of the Eurosceptic front rejecting the European Union's false European values, Wilders and Le Pen pitch re-establishing the "real" Europe as a political solution. The real Europe is characterized by its traditional values and must be defended from its enemies both foreign and domestic. Wilders's nationalism does not preclude his promotion of a Western identity. They are one of a piece. We must defend "our way of life" and "our traditional culture" (31), *our* meaning a singular Western culture; these values are pluralism, humaneness, democracy, and charity. Wilders looks to the Middle Ages for an example of what a muscular defence of a culture looks like, turning to the year 732 and the Frankish king Charles Martel's defeat of invading Islamic armies at the Battle of Tours, which in certain historical accounts, especially in eighteenth- and nineteenth-century scholarship, was a decisive, world-changing showdown between Christians and Muslims. According to these accounts, of which Gibbon's is the most well known, had the Franks lost, Europe would have been irrevocably changed, as Christianity might not have survived further Islamic conquests. Wilders surmises that when Charles Martel rallied his troops before the battle, he did not give "an Obama-style speech about them and us sharing the same values." For Wilders, "Christianity was saved in Europe solely because the people of Europe fought" (41); if the Franks had not stopped the advance of the Muslim armies in 732, today the West "would just be another poverty-stricken, underdeveloped colony of Islam" (57–58). The parallel between the early Middle Ages and today is made clear: we are in another 732 moment in the twenty-first century. The paradox Wilders presents is that the West is supremely humane and charitable but that these values must be militaristically and tenaciously defended. The "real history" of Europe is a narrative of a historical values-based community that we must defend like Charles Martel did almost 1,300 years ago.

Wilders is a leading figure among the far-right nationalist parties that have been increasing in influence and visibility (if not always power, though this too is increasing) throughout Europe for the last decade. In addition to Wilder's PVV and Le Pen's *Front National*, parties like the *Freiheitliche Partei Österreichs* (Freedom Party of Austria), *Alternative für Deutschland* (Alternative for Germany), and the UK Independent Party tout "traditional" values and national and cultural heritages, though perhaps none so forcefully as Jobbik. Jobbik, a far-right nationalist party in Hungary that has been rightfully charged with being anti-Semitic and anti-immigrant, claims that its "fundamental purpose is protecting Hungarian values and interests."[66] These values include a "Cultural programme," listed on its Principles webpage, which vows to protect and defend "ancient national symbols" and Hungary's "real ancient history." Jobbik promises to establish a Hungarian Ancient History Institute and endorses Kurultáj, a biennial event that began in 2008 as "a celebration of preservation of ancient traditions."[67] More than a ludic playground, Kurultáj explicitly seeks to revive ancient Hungarian traditions. It touts itself as "the largest celebration of the preservation of traditional heritage in Europe," and celebrates an ethnic Hun association of central Asians and eastern Europeans, from Bulgarians and Turks to Uzbeks and Mongolians. Celebrating horsemanship and crafts, Kurultáj extols medieval warrior skills like archery as its participants wear plate armour. Kurultáj offers its viewers a closed-circuit feed of ethnic history, nurturing an "authentic" strain of Hunnic culture.

Jobbik is an example of a political party that stands for a hardened nationalism where the nation is the prime source of the individual's identity. Each Hungarian citizen is encouraged to celebrate their history, a particular narrative that is told about triumph and heroism. Such triumphalism is touted as a "corrective" to the false memory of leftists who see only shame in the past and apologize for it. As a corrective to this false history, Jobbik promises to declare July 5 a national holiday to commemorate the victory of the Hungarian people at the Battle of Pressburg in 907, in which Hungarian forces defeated the East Francian army. Like Marine or Jean-Marie Le Pen using Clovis, Charlemagne, and Joan of Arc as medieval heroes who defended France against its enemies, or Geert Wilders turning to the eighth-century Battle of Tours to show what a vigorous and necessary defence of Europe against Muslims looks like, Jobbik exalts a triumphal vision of the medieval past for political gain. The revival and celebration of premodern pasts as fundamental to national and ethnic identity today is a lodestone of extremists on the right far beyond Jobbik and other political parties vying for power, as we have seen in the previous chapter.

The core of conservatism is the preservation and protection of what is perceived to be traditional. But as Anthony Giddens reminds us, tradition is dynamic and must be continually reinvented. Each generation rethinks the "traditional" to conform to new contexts and needs. However, even Giddens's acute analysis of the concept of tradition relies on a static, idealized Middle Ages. While

Giddens rightly notes that our notion of "tradition" is really the product of the last two centuries, he then says the concept did not exist "in medieval times [because] there was no generic notion of tradition. There was no call for such a word, precisely because tradition and custom were everywhere."[68] So, while Giddens's point is to show that "tradition" is a fairly recent concept, it is shown to be recent insofar as there was no concept of the new, and thus no concept of the traditional, in medieval society. The recent scholarship of Patricia Clare Ingham, however, dispels tired readings of the medieval as a time of conservation and seeks to rethink medieval writers as profoundly invested in problems with the new and the old.[69] Giddens's work, while certainly having important things to tell us about problems with tradition, still leans on the crutch that the Middle Ages were an immobile time that enjoyed and recognized traditions properly. Even here, the medieval is painted as a static time without innovation or invention.

Notes

[41] Roger Scruton, *How to Be a Conservative* (London: Bloomsbury, 2014), p. 1.

[42] See Mark C. Henrie, "Understanding Traditionalist Conservatism," in *Varieties of Conservatism in America*, ed. Peter Berkowitz (Stanford: Hoover Institution, 2004), pp. 3–30.

[43] Edmund Burke, *Reflections on the Revolution in France* (New York: Oxford University Press, 2009), p. 33.

[44] Zeev Sternhell, *The Anti-Enlightenment Tradition*, trans. David Maisel (New Haven: Yale University Press, 2009), pp. 194–95.

[45] Quoted in George H. Nash, *The Conservative Intellectual Movement in America Since 1945* (New York: Basic Books, 1976), p. 39.

[46] Richard Weaver, "Up from Liberalism," *Modern Age* 3 (Winter 1958–59): 30.

[47] Richard Weaver, *Ideas Have Consequences* (1948; Chicago: University of Chicago Press, 2013), p. 182. See also Weaver, "Southern Chivalry and Total War," *The Sewanee Review* 53 (1945): 267–78.

[48] Tison Pugh, *Queer Chivalry: Medievalism and the Myth of White Masculinity in Southern Literature* (Baton Rouge: LSU Press, 2013), p. 2.

[49] Russell Kirk, *America's British Culture* (New Brunswick: Transaction, 2005), pp. 92, 83.

[50] Russell Kirk, *The Roots of American Order* (Wilmington: Intercollegiate Studies Institute, 2003), p. 178.

[51] Rodney Stark, *How the West Won: The Neglected Story of the Triumph of Modernity* (Wilmington: Intercollegiate Studies Institute, 2014), p. 2.

[52] Rod Dreher, *Crunchy Cons: The New Conservative Counterculture and its Return to Roots* (New York: Three Rivers Press, 2006), pp. 245–47. See also Rod Dreher, *The Benedict Option: A Strategy for Christians in a Post-Christian Nation* (New York: Sentinel, 2017).

[53] Rod Dreher, "For a New Middle Age," *The American Conservative*, June 29, 2015, http://www.theamericanconservative.com/dreher/new-middle-ages-benedict-option-berdyaev/ (accessed July 7, 2016).

[54] William S. Lind and William S. Piper, "Alternate History," *American Conservative*, June 14, 2011, http://www.theamericanconservative.com/articles/alternate-history/ (accessed July 7, 2016).

[55] Patrick Buchanan, *The Death of the West: How Dying Populations and Immigrant Invasions Imperil Our Country and Civilization* (New York: St. Martin's, 2002), pp. 147–48.

[56] Patrick Buchanan, "'The Great White Hope,'" *buchanan.org*, May 26, 2016, http://buchanan.org/blog/great-white-hope-125286?utm_source=feedburner&utm_medium=twitter&utm_campaign=-Feed%3A+PatrickBuchanan+%28Pat+Buchanan+Update%29 (accessed June 28, 2016).

[57] Timothy Stanley, *The Crusader: The Life and Tumultuous Times of Pat Buchanan* (New York: St. Martin's Press, 2012), p. 238.

[58] M. Stanton Evans, *The Theme is Freedom: Religion, Politics, and the American Tradition* (Washington, DC: Regnery, 1994), p. xiii.

[59] See Eric Hobsbawm, "Introduction: Inventing Traditions," in *The Invention of Tradition*, ed. Eric Hobsbawm and Terrence Ranger (Cambridge: Cambridge University Press, 2012; 1st ed. 1983), pp. 1–14.

[60] https://www.britainfirst.org/statement-of-principles/ (accessed September 7, 2016).

[61] https://cornerstonegroup.wordpress.com/about/ (accessed October 1, 2016).

[62] Nick Gutteridge, "Nigel Farage: Vote Brexit to Take UK Back from 'Contemptible' Cameron and his Rich Cronies," *The Daily Express*, June 1, 2016, http://www.express.co.uk/news/politics/676013/Nigel-Farage-tote-Brexit-take-UK-back-Cameron-cronies-EU-referendum (accessed October 10, 2016).

[63] Marine Le Pen, trans. John Cullen, "After Brexit, the People's Spring is Inevitable," *New York Times*, June 28, 2016, https://www.nytimes.com/2016/06/28/opinion/marine-le-pen-after-brexit-the-peoples-spring-is-inevitable.html (accessed June 29, 2016).

[64] Kim Willsher, "Marine Le Pen's Confidence Vindicated by Front National Election Triumph," *The Guardian*, May 25, 2014, http://www.theguardian.com/world/2014/may/25/marine-le-pen-confi-dence-proves-vindicated-front-national (accessed August 1, 2015).

[65] https://www.theguardian.com/world/2014/may/25/marine-le-pen-confidence-proves-vindicated-front-national (accessed August 1, 2015).

[66] http://jobbik.com/short_summary_about_jobbik (accessed July 20, 2016).

[67] http://kurultaj.hu (accessed July 20, 2016).

[68] Anthony Giddens, *Runaway World: How Glabalization is Reshaping our Lives* (London: Profile, 2002), p. 39.

Chapter 4

Anxious Returns: The New Feudalism and New Medievalism

Enjoy your Servitude!

We are over a decade and a half into the twenty-first century, and feudalism has returned. In the stupor and shock of the hangover weeks after the Brexit vote in June 2016, segments of the digital vox populi howled with glee at the rejection of the neo-feudal European Union. It was the first peasants' revolt since 1381, a *Daily Telegraph* writer tweeted; giddy bloggers lauded the fall of the neo-feudal bankers; an Italian financial journalist riled up his audience on television by excitedly denouncing the neo-feudal authority and control of the European Union.[70] For some, the Brexit vote broke the chains of the descendant of an economic, social, and political system whose name is used synonymously with injustice, inequality, and unfairness: feudalism.

Neo-feudalism, or new feudalism—the terms are often used interchangeably to denote the return of feudalist society—appropriates the Middle Ages in an alternate form of dark medievalism. Thus far, this book has to a large degree explored the right's deployments of the medieval, but neo-feudalism is a primarily (though not exclusively) leftist model of the premodern past. If the far right and traditionalist conservatism laud a static idealized medieval, writers positing a global neo-feudalism fear a static anxiety-inducing medieval. Neo-feudalism as well as new medievalism, addressed later in this chapter, engage in dark medievalism by consistently and broadly painting the medieval as politically and socially primitive. As a term that emerged only in the nineteenth century to describe all of medieval European society, feudalism is a vexing and highly problematic concept used as shorthand for cataloguing and simplifying historical complexity. Neo-feudalism, then, is built upon very unstable foundations. The medieval is located as the site of injustice, inequality, and inhumanity, constantly threatening to invade and replace modern values. But the very concept of feudalism is itself a postmedieval idea, constructed to represent life before individual liberty and social justice.

Utilized to represent deep, inherent fractures in the framework of corporate capitalism, neo-feudalism is a free-ranging term. It is regularly dropped in mainstream media articles with titles such as "Slouching Towards Neo-feudalism" and "America: Home of the Bewildered Serf and Land of the Feudal Lords," both published at the *Huffington Post*. The writers of these articles are keen to present digestible definitions of the concept: neo-feudalism is said to be a signifier of "a system with two sets of rules, one for the rich and another for the poor."[71] Contemporary monopolistic capitalism is depicted as being like traditional feudal societies in that private interests have become more powerful than the government. Crony capitalism and corporate welfare become modern variants of feudal institutions, robbing individuals of their humanity. For incensed voices infuriated with the injustices and unfairness of crony capitalism, the working-class and middle-class consumers increasingly resemble disenfranchised medieval peasants, unable to resist exploitation and to defend their interests.

The idea of a new feudalism did not spontaneously emerge from the wake of the Brexit vote; rather, the return of feudalism is a concept that has increasingly taken hold over the last decade. One commentator leading the charge for the return of feudalism is Bruce Schneier, whose articles with titles such as "Power in the Age of the Feudal Internet" contend that power has been inequitably consolidated in the hands of a few major tech corporations like Facebook, Apple, and Google. This power imbalance has resulted in the empowerment of the few and the disempowerment of the many. As a non-specialist deploying simplified historical mirrors to help frame contemporary problems, Schneier wisely admits to the makeshift nature of his use of the term "feudal"—and then deploys it anyway. The definition of feudalism that Schneier offers can act as a useful way to understand how "feudalism" is conceived today in the popular imagination. For Schneier, feudalism is above all hierarchical, accompanied by a series of mutual obligations and a clear divide between haves and have-nots. Tech corporations are feudal lords and tech users are their vassals. It is all about control: as users we give up certain freedoms and liberties and in turn we are offered protection in the form of cybersecurity by Sir Apple. Mixing his medieval metaphors, Schneier laments that Robin Hood hackers who subvert the system cannot save us; instead, he calls for stronger government regulatory oversight over tech companies. The result will be like the fall of medieval feudalism: "the rise of the centralized state and the rule of law" finally put an end to medieval feudal society.[72] Power was concentrated in the hands of the few, unfairly and unjustly, until a more rational and lawful governmental body stepped in. Schneier calls for a twenty-first century Magna Carta to regulate and rein in oppressive corporate power.

In the last few years, Schneier's concept of a neo-feudalistic technocracy has taken hold as a kind of truth among tech journalists seeking to provide meaningful commentary on the way we live now. Neo-feudalism, though, is not restricted to the digital domain: it has come to signify the entirety of an unfair two-tier system, from the police to the judicial system to the economy. "Neo-feudal" has been used to describe the corporate state in totem, especially that of the United States. We are said to be living in nothing less than "an age of neo-feudalism," in which the game is rigged for the elite and against the masses.[73] The logical end of capitalism restarts a cycle to a return to pre-capitalist systems.

For those who call this an age of neo-feudalism, feudalism is synonymous with inequality and injustice. We "serfs" are mockingly implored to "just keep quiet, pay your debts, pay your lords's debts, use the service entrance and enjoy your servitude!"[74] The term "neo-feudalism" is flexible: it dates from the early 1960s as a charge against the left's support for what was seen as overbearing state interventions into individual's lives; later, in 1992, Immanuel Wallerstein suggested neo-feudalism as a potential substitute for historical capitalism when capitalist civilization meets its inevitable end. Wallerstein briefly defines neo-feudalism as a turn towards local, self-contained regions, but he does not elaborate the point.[75]

It is only since the Great Recession of 2008, though, that the phrase has become ubiquitous, especially with the rise of the Occupy Wall Street movement of 2011. Though it has dissipated as a cohesive movement, Occupy Wall Street launched in 2011 as a continuous protest in Zuccotti Park in downtown Manhattan, subsequently spreading to a number of other cities across the US and beyond. The protesters primarily targeted increasing global income inequality but also addressed other social justice issues, especially the student loan debt crisis. The term "neo-feudalism" became so prevalent during the peak of the

Occupy movement that there was a rally held entitled
March Against Neo-Feudalism: Revenge of the Wage Slave.
Neo-feudalism is deployed as shorthand for crony capitalism, signifying the problem of income inequality produced by an unfettered oligarchy ruling a disempowered
majority.[76] Corporate elites are charged with being above
the law and corporations are charged with wielding more
power than the state itself, at the expense of the masses.

Although warnings about our neo-feudalist way of life
emanate primarily from the left, voices on the right have
at times also assailed our increasingly neo-feudal world.
Writing for the *National Review* in 2014, Fred Bauer warns
about the power imbalance posed by neo-feudal tenden-
cies, but blames the identity politics of the left for caus-
ing divisiveness between different factions in the US. For
Bauer, "Present-day identity politics is the neofeudal version of [the medieval feudal] tradition."[77] In the medieval
feudal state, different classes were clearly disparate and
individuals saw themselves as part of a faction rather than
a larger nation; in such societies, justice was reserved
for the nobility and social divisions were insurmountable.
Today, neo-feudalism, led by identity politics separating
individuals by race, gender, sexuality, and ethnicity, con-
structs insurmountable walls around castes. Ultimately,
Bauer masks his attack on the "multiculturalist" politics of
the left with a critique of neo-feudalism, feigning an inter-
est in solving inequality and injustice as a pretense for condemning what he sees as cultural tribalism.

None of the articles and posts that I have read warning of a regression to a renewed version of feudalism are
interested in an engagement with the details of medieval
feudalism, let alone with the problem that feudalism as a
concept has been vexed from the earliest usages of the
term.[78] As with dark medievalism, historical context and
scholarly debates would only serve to muddy the useful-

ness of a facile concept. A sharp, definitive divide between lords and serfs is a powerful image. The website *Popular Resistance*, advertising Occupy Denver's March Against Neo-Feudalism, grounds its positions in a risibly vague history: "A few thousand years ago nobles and kings seized the commons from the peasants and called it private property. A few thousand years later similar excuses were used to wipe native populations off of Australia and The Americas in the name of God and progress."[79] Down with feudalism; down with all injustice and economic inequality. To be a neo-feudal state is to be a dichotomous state between haves and have-nots. History is shoved into line to serve its master.

California in particular is lamented as being the poster child for neo-feudalism, described by one writer as "a near-feudal society" inhabited by coastal elites and inland peasants.[80] For Joel Kotkin, perhaps the most vociferous of the ringers sounding the neo-feudal alarm, California is "practically medieval." The disappearance of a middle class in the twenty-first century has made an increasing number of Californians like medieval serfs, characterized by being downwardly mobile.[81] Just like "in medieval times, land ownership, particularly along the coast, has become increasingly difficult for those not in the upper class." Assuming Kotkin does not mean to compare medieval and modern coastal real estate, he is arguing that increasingly, only the California nobility is able to enjoy land ownership, as was the case with medieval nobility. "[M]odern day land serfs" pay the landlord's mortgage. Kotkin attempts to complicate a simplified have/have-not divide by classifying four castes in California: Oligarchs, Clerisy, New Serfs, and Yeomanry. This four-fold classification is obviously meant to neatly reflect the estate system of the three orders of the European Middle Ages. The Oligarchy are the landed aristocracy of technocrats and other billionaires; the Clerisy are the policy and ideas makers who keep others in line ideologically; the New Serfs are the powerless, landless, voiceless working class; and the Yeomanry are disappearing middle-class professionals. It is clear that Kotkin is not interested in detailing the actual historical circumstances of the Middle Ages, at times making frustratingly misguided statements, such as referring to "the old Third Estate in early medieval times," for example. It should be noted that it is not strictly true that the nobility owned all the land in medieval Europe, at least in medieval England, as the clergy were major landowners; nor is it entirely true that peasants were powerless and impoverished. Nonetheless, Kotkin's analogies reveal how some non-specialists conceive European society in the millennium before the seventeenth century.

One particularly colourful example of a mangled depiction of medieval society can be found at *The Amendment Gazette*, a blog dedicated to overturning the Citizens United Supreme Court case in the US.[82] An infographic[83] is titled "Feudalism Then & Now." It features a pyramid of the kind that one might find in a history textbook about feudalism. On the left side of the pyramid is Medieval Feudalism and on the right is Corporate Feudalism. At the tip of the pyramid is the .00001% of the population, at the rank of Monarchs on the left and Central Bankers on the right. Below the top rank are Landed Gentry/Big Bankers (.0001%), Clergy/Corporate Elite (.35%), the Royal Ministers/Elected Officials (.2%), Merchants/Top Bureaucrats (.2%), Vassals/Top Professionals (.75%), and Everyone Else/Everyone Else (98.5%). In miniscule letters at the bottom of the image is an attribution citing the US Census & Bureau of Labor Statistics; there is no citation for the Medieval Feudalism side. But the images used for the Medieval Feudalism side are the real giveaway for the shabbiness of the comparison. An icon of Henry VIII is used for the Monarchical class, the Lord Chamberlain Charles Sackville, who lived in the late seventeenth century, for the Landed Gentry; Lancelot Blackburne, the archbishop of York in the mid-eighteenth century, for the Clergy; Thomas Cromwell for the Royal Ministers; Christopher Columbus for the Merchants; Admiral Nelson for the Vassals; and medieval peasants from *Monty Python and the Holy Grail*. Other than Columbus, the only "medieval" representative in the pyramid is a modern spoof of the Middle Ages. Everyone else hails from the sixteenth to eighteenth centuries. Every figure on the right side of the image, the Corporate Feudalists, are contemporary political and corporate leaders, from Barack Obama to Ben Bernanke. The modern equivalent of the medieval peasants are the Simpsons.

The "medieval" and "feudal" are used unthinkingly as representatives of anything that seems absurdly outdated: powdered wigs, the tricorn hat, peasants in brown tattered rags, the luxurious, feathered cap of Henry VIII. Everything before the nineteenth century is thrown into a basket as "back then," and the premodern is reflexively unjust and unfair while the modern's core values of justice and fairness are threatened by nefarious corporate actors with an atavistic streak. The need to cite statistics for corporate dominance, without any apparent need to cite statistics for the medieval system, demonstrates the care that is given to historical analysis or accuracy. They simply do not matter. The "Feudalism Then & Now" image made the rounds on forums and blogs in the middle of 2016. It was posted on Reddit on the subreddits r/politicalrevolution and—tellingly, predictably—r/conspiracy.

Although this short book is not quite the place for a thorough study of the problems with feudalism as a concept, a few words here are necessary to briefly refute some of the superficial depictions of it that I have been examining. That the general public consistently misunderstands and misuses the word "feudalism" is old news, made familiar by E. A. R. Brown's landmark article in 1974 that examined the term's multifarious uses. Although the word "feudal" was used as early as the seventeenth century, the concept of medieval society as a fundamentally feudal system really came into being in the nineteenth century, and the earliest usage of the word "feudalism" only dates from 1839. It was then that the term came to represent a way of thinking about the Middle Ages's entire social, economic, and political system. Medieval people did not call their society a feudal one. This idea, like so many modern conceptions of the medieval period, derives from and is a reflection of eighteenth- and nineteenth-century thought. The word "feudal," in the Latin form *feodum*, or fief, was used in the Middle Ages in a strict sense, referring to a parcel of property in the form of real estate. Even if fiefs, vassalage, and mutual obligations were aspects of Western European society from roughly 1000–1500, medieval texts themselves do not quite go so far as to suggest that feudalism was the central organizing principle of society. It is only in postmedieval writings that historians came to see an entire society as wholly defined by its feudal obligations. As Brown pointedly argued forty years ago and as built upon by Susan Reynolds twenty years ago, historians tend to disregard, dismiss, or ignore documents that do not fit an ideal or a model. Feudalism was used to describe the social state of a whole era, taking feudal economic and martial obligations, loyalties, the administration of justice, and governmental structures and applying them to the whole of society. After the mid-nineteenth century, feudalism became a quick and easy way of "getting" the Middle Ages, at the expense of whatever evidence did not fit the mould.

As we have seen in the first chapter with dark medievalism and torture, the Middle Ages often perform as a facile proxy for injustice, inequality, intolerance, and unfairness. This bleak picture of the period may sometimes be the result of innocent ignorance, but even then it still carries with it political implications about the premodern past. In other cases, though, the medieval is consciously deployed as a political strategy. Susan Reynolds has shown how the French Revolution, for example, loaded with a desire to assign to the Middle Ages "whatever seemed most irrational and oppressive about the Ancien Régime, like the classification of society into distinct orders with a defined and legally privileged nobility" (8) stratified medieval and modern as an analogue for the old unjust order and the new order. After the Revolution, the most important thinker to solidify modern conceptions of a definitively pre-capitalist feudal age was Marx, who calcified the idea of different stages of history into a feudalism stage that came before and led to the capitalism stage.

When the Occupy movement and the Left denounce neo-feudalism, it is to some degree Marx's (or Marxism's) concept of feudalism that they are denouncing. The historical stages of ownership for Marx are tribal ownership, then communal or State ownership, then feudal, followed by modern private ownership. Feudal ownership of property arose with the decline of Roman power in the West. It instituted an inherently imbalanced system where hierarchical land ownership, as well as the feudal organization of urban trades, empowered the nobility, whom Marx calls a "robber-nobility," over serfs, whom Marx calls "a subjected producing class."[84] This describes, of course, Marx's dialectic divide between the empowered and disempowered.

Marx is clear that modern bourgeois society evolved from medieval feudal society, not merely temporally, but socially and economically, as the "two great hostile camps" of modern society, the Bourgeoisie and the Proletariat, are condensations of medieval urban merchants on the one hand and serfs on the other.[85] However, Marx does allow a certain complex division of classes in medieval town and country (princes, nobility, clergy, and peasants in the country and masters, journeymen, apprentices, and casual labourers in towns) that becomes condensed in modern capitalist society. As at any point since the ancient world, there existed a division between subjected and subjecter, but it was only in the modern period, after the sixteenth century, that the great class divide became class antagonists facing off against each other. Although the feudal serf developed into the proletariat and the medieval burgher into the modern bourgeoisie, Marx allows premodern societies a level of social complexity—"a complicated arrangement of society into various orders" (35)—that cannot be found in the modern world. Individuals were bound to each other in a more natural way than in capitalist society, and even if it was a society filled with ostentatious displays of overzealous piety and chivalry, at least those sentimental passions allowed for a kind of organic and personable relationship between individuals, as opposed to the hypocritical and "naked, shameless, direct, brutal exploitation" of modern capitalism. And yet, despite the complicated class arrangement that Marx draws of the medieval period and the admiration (however brief) with which he and Engels describe it, feudal society is nevertheless the soil from which capitalist society grew. Holsinger and Knapp have identified this paradox about the Middle Ages in Marx's thought: it is a "prelapsarian pastoral" and yet it sowed the seeds for the full-bore exploitation of industrial capitalism.[86] The dissolution of feudal economies for Marx liberated the elements of capitalist society.

Marx ascribes a simple progressive line from feudal to free as a bourgeois historian's way of thinking. Feudal labourers did become freer as sellers of their own labour-power after breaking free of the labour regulations of the guilds and land-bound rural serfdom, but Marx insists that labour's movement towards greater freedom entailed a total loss of their own means of production. Modern wage-labourers do not form any part of the means of production, as a serf or slave would, and do not own the means of production, as would a self-employed peasant. The newly "freed" labourers of capitalist society are transformed from producers to wage-labourers by selling their time. Marx draws a clear line between the feudal era and the modern era by stating emphatically that the capitalist era begins with the sixteenth century.

Even if Marx's thought on precapitalist society is astronomically more complex than some commentators today cautioning about a new feudalism, he nonetheless maintains a sharp divide between feudalism and capitalism and insists that the one developed into the other. The burgeoning potential of capitalism in feudal economies—that feudal society harboured primitive elements of capitalist society—is an important element for those warning about post-capitalist returns to feudalism today. A blog called *The Progressive Cynic* feverishly worried in 2014 about how "ironic [it is] that our country was built as an alternative to the old tradition of monarchy and feudalism, yet many Americans today are running back to that type of government willingly."[87] This is an inherent fear of the neo-feudal harbingers: that capitalism will revert to its feudal precursor, a more vicious, unpredictable, and immature socio-economic model of itself. Marx is by no means singlehandedly responsible for the simplification and ubiquity of feudalism as the easy answer for what came before capitalism, but the colossal impact of his thought cannot be overstated. Even if he did offer some nuance to the feudal model, Marx never developed a coherent and comprehensive analysis of medieval economies, and his picture of the period was not quite developed over the course of his career. The period remains static in his thought.[88]

It is this stasis, in a sense, which dominates the discourse of neo-feudalism today. The feudal represents the non-dynamic, the fundamentally unjust and unequal. Even if he is clear about when the transition happened, Marx's lack of clarity about how the transition from feudalism to capitalism occurred clears the way for others to imagine a reverse transition: that we progressed to capitalism and could just as easily fall back to feudalism. Although Marx is ultimately somewhat sympathetic with certain aspects of feudal societies that he thought were relatively laudable compared with the evils of industrial capitalism, the overarching structure of his historical model remains a feudal economy that stretched from the dissipation of the Roman Empire to the sixteenth century. It involved, broadly speaking, a bipartite societal division between those with and those without power and agency.

Some cautionary voices on neo-feudalism reject Marx's historical framework of feudalism-capitalism-communism because feudalism never fully evolved into industrial capitalism. For political philosopher Ronald W. Dworkin, since the Middle Ages feudalism has been and is still part of the West's economic structure. History is not a progressive line forward but an undulation back and forth from feudalism to capitalism. This is "Our Feudal Moment," Dworkin declares in a section heading of his recent book *How Karl Marx Can Save American Capitalism*, because a series of modern "guilds" and regulations stops small businesses and individuals from maximizing their potential productivity. This is something of a Tea Party argument (Dworkin worked at the Hudson Institute, a conservative think-tank), in that it blames the bureaucracy of government and corporate overreach for stymieing freedom and holding back the full potential of an unleashed American economy. Marx was wrong, according to Dworkin, to believe that feudalism was dead and buried; it is still "a viable alternative to democracy."[89] "Feudalism is fear—intense fear," Dworkin writes, resulting in a total lack of independence for the powerless and social, political, and economic relationships that are built on fear, so much so that American workers today exist in "a great chain of fear" (158). Feudalism is the festering wound in capitalism's otherwise healthy body, crooked and unproductive. This is the neo-feudalism of the right: a libertarian term used to signify a pure, unfettered entrepreneurial market that has been corrupted by corporate monopolies, whereas the left uses the term to signify capitalism as a lost cause.

The neo-feudal state is characterized by a fundamental inequality manifested as an acute divide between haves and have-nots, by downwardly mobile serfdom for most of the population, by corporate control of the state, by land ownership restricted to an aristocracy, and by a clear-cut caste system sharply delineating lines between different socioeconomic groups. But, unfortunately for a simplistic neo-feudalism that proposes a sharp divide between corporate lord and consumer serf, the realities of medieval feudalism were much too complex for facile explanations, just as capitalism or communism are easily caricatured but not easily understood in depth.

New Medievalism: Anxiety and Disorder

Neo-feudalism can be viewed as a more aggressive version of new medievalism, a concept in international relations theory that had its heyday towards the end of the twentieth century. If neo-feudalism is especially concerned with finance, economics, and social justice on an individual scale, new medievalism is a macro-political and macro-economic model of statelessness. New medievalism can be viewed as a more scholarly reflection of neo-feudalism's anxiety about global disorder, though with its focus on political systems rather than income inequality and social justice. Yet, like the commentators on neo-feudalism, some new medievalism theorists share "reversion" fears—that the modern world is in danger of sinking back into the dark days of feudalism. As with neo-feudalism, new medievalism is often (though not always) packaged with warnings of chaos. The medieval is linked with anxiety, fear, unrest, and violence. In both neo-feudalism and new medievalism, the medieval gets misconstrued through over-simplification to fit political schemes which stoke fear and anxiety, because the medieval is itself representative of fear and anxiety. Both neo-feudalism and new medievalism on the whole are based on inadequate historical understanding of the premodern past. They fail to see how the "feudal" and the "medieval" were both constructed as modern ideas.

Introduced in 1962 by Arnold Wolfers[90] and revisited and re-evaluated in 1977 by Australian international relations theorist Hedley Bull in his book *The Anarchical Society*, new medievalism posits that the key characteristics of medieval political order were "overlapping authority and multiple loyalty"[91] and that the international state system of the latter half of the twentieth century is returning to a pluricentric stateless model of entangled authorities. No state or single ruler held true sovereignty in the Middle Ages, new medievalism holds, insofar as all sovereignty was shared between local (such as a monarch) and world (the Holy Roman Empire or the Church) authorities. Although Bull is ultimately agnostic on the subject of whether the modern world is in fact returning to a new form of a medieval political order, he discusses the possibility that the late twentieth century witnessed a re-emergence of a medieval political order.

This re-emergence was due to sovereignty being shared between local and global authorities like a pan-European federation (such as the European Economic Community, a precursor of the European Union in Bull's day), the United Nations, or, from the mid-1990s, the World Trade Organization. The elements of new medievalism categorized by Bull are the disintegration of the traditional nation-state, whether into smaller, hyper-regionalized linguistic and ethnic states or into larger international bodies (such as the European Economic Community); a shift away from Max Weber's definition of the state as that which monopolizes the right to use legitimate force and towards the accepted violence of guerillas and terrorists; and increased political and economic power of multinational corporations and international institutions like the World Bank.

Wolfers's and Bull's new medievalism was something of a shot in the dark. They do not explore the Middle Ages in any real depth. Even the writer of the foreword to the Fourth Edition of *The Anarchical Society* admits that Bull's discussion of new medievalism is underdeveloped. After *The Anarchical Society*, new medievalism fell by the wayside until the 1990s, when it was reinvigorated by historians such as Alain Minc and international relations scholars such as Stephen Kobrin. Perhaps fear of a "return" to disorder was due to an apocalyptic panic brought on by millennialism and the Y2K hysteria.[92] A more likely scenario, however, is that there arose a prevailing sense among some intellectuals in the 1990s that the nation state was breaking down irreparably and that tribalism was coming to replace nationalism. Most medievalists will be familiar with Umberto Eco's essays on the return of the Middle Ages published in the mid-1970s, which diagnose an inherent psychological desire for the medieval as a quest for origins. But the return of the medieval in the 1990s among certain scholarly circles was driven primarily by hyperbolic fears of violence, disorder, and chaos in cities and on a global level. Alain Minc, for instance, warns readers in his 1993 book *Le nouveau Moyen Âge* of a relapse into a superstitious, chaotic world in turmoil not seen since the Middle Ages; a modern world, like the medieval one, where states are borderless and run by lawless barons, and the ordered world of discreet sovereign nation-states has collapsed.

Fear had been entrenched at the core of new medievalism all along. Even if Bull does not fully embrace new medievalism as a theory, his argument in *The Anarchical Society* is an explicit defence of the states system. He hopes to slow or stop the decline of the international states system, because what lies on the other side is unknowable, unfamiliar, and chaotic. New medievalism models entail a breakdown of the state's monopoly on the legitimate use of violence by insurgents and terrorists. Such "sub-state actors," as Chris Berzins and Patrick Cullen call them, are a crucial factor in the emergence of an international new medievalism, a political situation that further propitiates the spread of terrorism.[93] Some more recent scholarship has been more vehement about using a medieval political framework as a representative of an unjust and primitive system that looms over the modern states system as a sort of bogeyman. Setting up a clash between corporate oligarchies and ethnic tribalism, in his popular 1995 book *Jihad vs. McWorld* political scientist Benjamin Barber warns of "an atavistic return to medieval politics," with the universal Church and isolated fiefdoms represented today by the clashing forces of the global marketplace and disruptive tribal identities.[94] The medieval was a "world of status, hierarchy, and popular ignorance." The return to the atavistic medieval would turn people back into feudal bondsmen without any rights.

In general, most non-medievalists working in international relations or political science do not cast as negative a mould over the Middle Ages as that. Most scholarship from non-medievalists has been significantly more circumspect and reserved about making grandiose or overweening claims about the medieval period. A new volume has been published, *Medieval Foundations of International Relations* (2017), which collects essays that offer a fuller picture of the Middle Ages than Bull or Winn.[95] The essays aim to reveal the period's importance to modern international relations rather than spotlight its enduring otherness. Nevertheless, the frequent application of terms like "fragmented," "ambiguous," "breakdown," and "disintegration" to describe the premodern political situation of Western Europe belies an anxiety about a reversion to such uncertainty today.

Most international relations theorists maintain that new medievalism is a useful analogical construct, a "loose parallel" (22) as Berzins and Cullen put it, rather than a literal, precise historiographical comparison. But new medievalism as a theory has extended well beyond its analogical scope in academia, as Bruce Holsinger has argued. In the aftermath of 9/11, new medievalism went mainstream in the United States. It began informing policy discourse among think tanks and governmental bodies, appearing in widely read periodicals like *Foreign Affairs* and *The Atlantic*. In that transition from the academy to the Department of Defense and neoconservative thinkers, the overlapping and intersecting structures of medieval political power—the "breakdown," "fracturing," "disintegration," and stateless violence associated with premodern (dis)order—became equated with Islamist terrorist organizations and with failed states like Afghanistan. Afghanistan has recently been likened to a medieval state embroiled in "medieval power politics," incapable of cohering into and thriving as a modern, centralized state.[96] In order to make the medieval analogy work, the entirety of the medieval millennium must be boiled down to a few exaggerated suppo-sitions—fragmentation, decentralization, theocracy, holy war—with the unexamined medieval being little more than a rhetorical strategy. As Holsinger puts it, American neoconservatives after 9/11 deployed new medievalism by "exploiting it, and using it to their own tactical advan-tage."[97] At the time, Al-Qaeda was cast as violent stateless neomedievals revolting against the hegemony of the mod-ern Western nation-state. There are new stateless ghosts of the medieval past, especially the Islamic State, as the first chapter suggests. They are perceived to be such both by their enemies and by themselves.

Notes

[69] Patricia Clare Ingham, *The Medieval New: Ambivalence in an Age of Innovation* (Philadelphia: University of Pennsylvania Press, 2015).

[70] Christopher Hope, Twitter Post, June 23, 2016, 11:00 p.m., https://twitter.com/christopherhope/status/746176216688910336 (accessed August 10, 2016); https://mpbondblog.wordpress.com/2016/08/01/brexit-and-neo-feudalism/ (accessed October 15, 2016); Ross Logan, "Italian Journalist Destroys Anti-Brexit Arguments and Blasts 'Rubbish' EU," *The Daily Express*, June 27, 2016, http://www.express.co.uk/news/uk/683556/Italian-journalist-destroys-anti-Brexit-arguments-blasts-European-Union (accessed September 10, 2016).

[71] Garrett Johnson, "Slouching Towards Neofeudalism," *Huffington Post*, May 25, 2011, http://www.huffingtonpost.com/garrett-johnson/slouching-towards-neofeud_b_568972.html (accessed August 8, 2016).

[72] Bruce Schneier, "The Battle for Power on the Internet," *The Atlantic*, October 24, 2014, https://www.theatlantic.com/technology/archive/2013/10/the-battle-for-power-on-the-internet/280824/ (accessed September 11, 2016).

[73] John W. Whitehead, "The Age of Neo-feudalism: A Government of the Rich, by the Rich and for the Corporations," *Huffington Post*, March 30, 2013, http://www.huffingtonpost.com/john-w-whitehead/the-age-of-neofeudalism_b_2566546.html (accessed June 26, 2016).

[74] Dave Pederson, "America: Home of the Bewildered Serf and Land of the Feudal Lords," *Huffington Post*, July 4, 2012, http://www.huffingtonpost.com/dave-pederson/america-home-of-the-bewil_b_1476594.html (accessed June 26, 2016).

[75] Immanuel Wallerstein, *Historical Capitalism with Capitalist Civilization* (London: Verso, 2003), p. 162.

[76] Majia Holmer Nadesan, "Neofeudalism and the Financial Crisis: Implications for Occupy Wall Street," in *Understanding Occupy from Wall Street to Portland: Applied Studies in Communication Theory*, ed. Renee Guarriello Heath, Courtney Vail Fletcher, and Ricardo Munoz (Lanham: Lexington, 2013), p. 36.

[77] Fred Bauer, "The New Feudalism," *The National Review*, July 9, 2014, http://www.nationalreview.com/article/382266/new-feudalism-fred-bauer (accessed August 8, 2016).

[78] See E. A. R. Brown, "The Tyranny of a Construct: Feudalism and Historians of Medieval Europe," *The American Historical Review*

79 (1974): 1063–88; and Susan Reynolds, *Fiefs and Vassals: The Medieval Evidence Reinterpreted* (1996; New York: Oxford University Press, 2001).

[79] https://www.popularresistance.org/occupydenvermarchagainstneo-feudalismrevengeofthewageslave/ (accessed August 9, 2016).

[80] Conn Carroll, "California Becoming a Feudal Society," *Washington Examiner*, March 2, 2013, http://www.washingtonexaminer.com/conn-carroll-california-becoming-a-feudal-society/article/2522998 (accessed August 8, 2016).

[81] Joel Kotkin, "California'a New Feudalism Benefits a Few at the Expense of the Multitude," *The Daily Beast*, October 5, 2013, http://www.thedailybeast.com/articles/2013/10/05/california-s-new-feudalism-benefits-a-few-at-the-expense-of-the-multitude.html (accessed August 8, 2016).

[82] In the 2010 case *Citizens United v. Federal Elections Commission*, the Supreme Court ruled by a vote of 5–4 that nonprofit corporations could not be restricted in their financial support of political candidates. In short, the ruling defined money as a form of free speech. The case has been enormously controversial, especially among the American left, for its influence on corporate control of the political sphere. See http://i0.wp.com/www.amendmentgazette.com/wp-content/uploads/2013/08/feudalism_then_now.jpg (accessed January 10, 2017).

[83] http://i0.wp.com/www.amendmentgazette.com/wp-content/uploads/2013/08/feudalism_then_now.jpg (accessed September 5, 2017).

[84] Karl Marx, *The German Ideology* (Amherst: Prometheus Books, 1998), p. 40.

[85] Karl Marx and Friedrich Engels, *The Communist Manifesto: A Modern Edition* (London: Verson, 2012), p. 35.

[86] Bruce Holsinger and Ethan Knapp, "The Marxist Premodern," *Journal of Medieval and Early Modern Studies* 34 (2004): 464–65.

[87] Josh Sager, "Neo-Feudalism Captures the United States," *Progressive Cynic*, May 13, 2014, https://theprogressivecynic.com/2014/05/13/neo-feudalism-captures-the-united-states/ (accessed August 30, 2016).

[88] See John H. Pryor, "Karl Marx and the Medieval Economy," https://openjournals.library.sydney.edu.au/index.php/ART/article/viewFile/5564/6232 (accessed September 12, 2016).

[89] M. W. D. Dworkin, *How Karl Marx Can Save American Capitalism* (London: Lexington Books, 2015), p. 157.

[90] Arnold Wolfers, *Discord and Collaboration: Essays on International*

Politics (1962; Baltimore: The Johns Hopkins University Press, 1991), p. 242.

[91] Hedley Bull, *The Anarchical Society*, 4th ed. (New York: Columbia University Press, 2012), p. 245.

[92] Y2K was a computer bug that was anticipated to cause potentially major problems when computers would not be able to distinguish between the years 1900 and 2000; it wound up affecting very few computer systems. Christopher Frayling, "The Strange Allure of the Middle Ages," *The Independent*, May 27, 1995, http://www.independent.co.uk/voices/the-strange-allure-of-the-middle-ages-1621518.html (accessed September 7, 2016).

[93] Chris Berzins and Patrick Cullen, "Terrorism and Neo-Medievalism," in *Neo-Medievalism and Civil Wars*, ed. Neil Winn (London: Frank Cass, 2004), p. 9.

[94] Benjamin Barber, *Jihad vs. McWorld: How Globalism and Tribalism are Reshaping the World* (New York: Ballantine Books, 1996), p. 7.

[95] *Medieval Foundations of International Relations*, ed. William Bain (London: Routledge, 2017).

[96] Thomas Barfield, "Is Afghanistan 'Medieval'?," *Foreign Policy*, June 2, 2010, http://foreignpolicy.com/2010/06/02/is-afghanistan-medieval-2/ (accessed April 24, 2017).

Postscript

The Eternal Return of the Medieval

Sometimes both sides of a political divide will deploy the medieval as a conceptual weapon. We can see both sides of the political medieval—the medieval as crucial heritage and dark medievalism—in Slobodan Milošević, the former President of Yugoslavia and Serbia indicted for war crimes by the International Court of Justice at The Hague. In his infamous Gazimestan speech on June 28, 1989, given at an event to commemorate the 600th anniversary of the Battle of Kosovo, a 1389 battle between invading Ottoman Turks and Serbian forces, Milošević's speech, which is generally considered to have helped instigate the ethnic cleansing and bloodshed that would soon destroy thousands of lives, referred to the battle as "an event of the distant past which has great historical and symbolic significance for its future."[98] The event, for Milošević, is distant enough that it is not important to distinguish between what is true and what is legendary about the battle, or even whether the Serbians won or lost to the Ottomans. "If" the Serbians lost, it was due in large part to the disunity of the Serbian people, which Milošević then uses to call for solidarity and unity today. What Milošević is doing, of course, is calling for ethnic solidarity against the enemy other. In 1389, Serbians "regarded disunity as its greatest disaster. Therefore it is the obligation of the people to remove disunity, so that they may protect themselves from defeats, failures, and stagnation in the future." As with traditionalist conservatism as well as more extreme variants of the right, here again is a fantasy of medieval ideals of ethnic and racial solidarity and communal identity, and the call for such a communal identity today. Consider the ethnic cleansing that was about to happen against Islamic Albanians in Kosovo. Milošević ended his speech by saying that Serbia in 1389 was defending not just itself but Europe; Serbia was the "bastion that defended the European culture, religion, and European society in general." Here, again, is a kind of European racial community defending itself against the Muslim foreigner. The fourteenth-century battle between Christian Serbian and Muslim Ottoman Turk is deployed as a jingoist call to arms. To rally his people and consolidate his power, the vicious tyrant Milošević draped himself in medievalism.[99]

After the war, Milošević's trial at The Hague opened with a tinge of dark medievalism. Carla del Ponte, one of the chief prosecutors, began the trial by saying, "Some of the incidents revealed an almost medieval savagery and a calculated cruelty that went far beyond the bounds of legitimate warfare."[100] To both Milošević and Del Ponte, the medieval is synonymous with violence: for the one, a heroic and romantic violence; for the other, a barbaric and feral violence—but violence nonetheless. Why it should be a medieval savagery, rather than the patently obvious modern savagery that it is, reveals the walls that modernity builds around itself to keep out what it does not want to see.

The Middle Ages are always returning. They returned in the 1700s, as we saw with the thought of Burke in Chapter 3; they returned in the 1800s in literature, architecture, and the visual arts; they returned in the 1960s and 1970s with new medievalism in international relations theory, as we saw with Wolfers and Bull in Chapter 4; they returned in the 2010s with neo-feudalism; and they returned again with Donald Trump's calls for "medieval"-like torture procedures and so-called black sites.

It is crucial to not make overwrought and blind assumptions and generalizations about alternative forms to contemporary dominant systems and institutions. Doing so potentially limits ways of thinking outside of our financial and political systems, reducing the field of potential alternatives or solutions to inherent and manufactured problems with global capitalism. The study of history matters, not just for the sake of itself, but because it can provide useful alternative models to contemporary systems and ideas. At the same time, it is important for scholars, especially for the kinds of scholars like medievalists, whose areas of expertise are often the subject of popular representations, not to avert their eyes from the popular.

The popular is political.[101] If grossly oversimplified historical analogues go unimpeded and unchallenged, we potentially cede critical political space to extremist elements. Consider Daniel Friberg, the far-right CEO of Arktos publishing, for example, which publishes fascist, neo-Nazi drivel. I have had the distinct displeasure of studying Arktos's catalogue over the last few years, as they publish a number of the extremist materials studied in this book and in my previous work. Friberg has recently written a book that applauds the Holy Roman Empire for allowing a greater degree of autonomy and freedom to its various regions than is allowed to modern nation-states under the European Union. "Looking back before the world of liberalism"—before the modern world—"presents us with revolutionary ideas," Friburg writes.[102] The revolutionary potential in premodern European society ought to be something worthy of serious study. But when that potential is being deployed towards extremist, fascist, white-supremacist ends, then scholars must act to counter such vicious manipulation.

During the weekend of the inauguration of Donald Trump as the 45th American president, the leaders of a number of prominent far-right European political parties gathered in Koblenz to celebrate and strategize. They openly glorified the dawning of a new world, one that they have been working to create, that has come into being. This is a world in which people awaken to the reality and meanings of their white European identity—which includes North Americans, as we have seen. In 2017, white identity is centre stage. A lodestone of that identity is the heritage and legacy of the Middle Ages, which are perceived by many on the far and extreme right to be the bedrock of national and racial origins. Anyone who seriously studies the Middle Ages should be vigilant.

Notes

[97] Bruce Holsinger, *Neomedievalism, Neoconservatism, and the War on Terror* (Chicago: Prickly Paradigm, 2007), p. 65.

[98] https://cmes.arizona.edu/sites/cmes.arizona.edu/files/SLOBO-DAN%20Milošević_speech_6_28_89.pdf (accessed January 16, 2017).

[99] A point that was well made by Michael Dobbs, "Milošević: Wrapped in Medieval Mettle," *Washington Post*, March 28, 1999, https://www.washingtonpost.com/archive/opinions/1999/03/28/Milošević-wrapped-in-medieval-mettle/16a51405-fd95-4551-b90b-2e7513a8cecf/?utm_term=.e22ffd02b21a (accessed January 10, 2017).

[100] "Del Ponte's Words: 'An Almost Medieval Savagery'," *New York Times*, February 3, 2002, http://www.nytimes.com/2002/02/13/world/del-ponte-s-words-an-almost-medieval-savagery.html (accessed June 8, 2016).

[101] Thanks to my friend and colleague Sucheta Kanjilal for this pithy phrase.

[102] Daniel Friberg, *The Real Right Returns: A Handbook for the True Opposition* (London: Arktos, 2015), p. x.

Further Reading

With a few exceptions that are pivotal to the study of political medievalism, these are books and articles that have not been cited already. I have selected texts that either address political medievalism head-on or that draw upon the medieval as a key part of discussions of larger issues. This list is not meant to be comprehensive. It is intended to act as a starting point for any reader interested in pursuing some of the ideas and problems elicited by this book. Note that there is some extremist material here, and in no way do I mean to promote any ideas in these particular writings. Nevertheless, they can be worth studying for readers who want to understand extremist medievalism.

Bar-On, Tamir. *Rethinking the French New Right: Alternatives to Modernity*. London: Routledge, 2013.

> Studies the far-right French *Nouvelle Droite*, examining recent trends in nationalism and identity among the French and European right.

Benoist, Alain de and Charles Champetier. *Manifesto for a European Renaissance*. London: Arktos, 2012.

> The far-right political philosopher de Benoist has penned numerous articles and books, but for a sort of primer on his thought, this is a good start. In short, de Benoist describes modernity as a secular Middle Ages.

Bornschier, Simon. *Cleavage Politics and the Populist Right: The New Cultural Conflict in Western Europe*. Philadelphia: Temple University Press, 2010.

> Examines populist right parties in Europe that contrast libertarian-universalistic values with their own traditionalist-communitarian values as such parties have increasingly turned to identity politics.

The Cambridge Companion to Medievalism. Edited by Louise D'Arcens. Cambridge: Cambridge University Press, 2016.

> Entries on nationalism (Utz), warfare (Lynch), and neo-medievalism and international relations (Holsinger) are particularly useful for studying political medievalism.

Dreher, Rod. *The Benedict Option: A Strategy for Christians in a Post Christian Nation*. New York: Sentinel, 2017.

> Dreher's most recent book continues his determination to pursue a countercultural brand of Christian activism that is rooted in medieval figures and ideas.

Elliott, Andrew B. R. *Medievalism, Politics, and Mass Media*. Cambridge: Brewer, 2017.

> From Anders Breivik to al-Qaeda to the English Defence League, examines how medievalism affects our understanding of contemporary politics.

Friedrichs, Jörg. "The Meaning of New Medievalism." *European Journal of International Relations* 7 (2001): 475–502.

> Offers a balanced overview of new medievalism, maintaining that dichotomous breaks between medieval chaos and modern order are wrong-headed.

Ganim, John M. *Medievalism and Orientalism: Three Essays on Literature, Architecture, and Cultural Identity*. New York: Palgrave Macmillan, 2005.

> A short but influential and important book that shows how medievalism functions like orientalism.

Geary, Patrick. *The Myth of Nations: The Medieval Origins of Europe*. Princeton: Princeton University Press, 2002.

A vital study refuting misconceptions about national origins, myths, and identities.

Holsinger, Bruce. *Neomedievalism, Neoconservatism, and the War on Terror*. Chicago: Prickly Paradigm, 2007.

A brief but crucial introduction to political medievalism after 9/11.

International Medievalism and Popular Culture. Edited by Louise D'Arcens and Andrew Lynch. Amherst: Cambria Press, 2014.

Studies intersections between globalism, international relations, and popular and political medievalisms.

Judis, John B. *The Populist Explosion: How the Great Recession Transformed American and European Politics*. New York: Columbia Global Reports, 2016.

Despite the subtitle, offers a brief but handy introduction to a history of populism in the US since the late nineteenth century and discusses the rise of populist politics in Europe and the US today.

Mastnak, Tomaž. "Europe and the Muslims: A Permanent Crusade?." In *The New Crusades: Constructing the Muslim Enemy*, edited by Emran Qureshi and Michael A. Sells, pp. 205–48. New York: Columbia University Press, 2003.

Argues that hostility towards the Muslim world played a key role in the formation of the idea of Europe as a political unit and that there remains a permanent crusade against Muslims.

Matthews, David. *Medievalism: A Critical History*. Cambridge: Brewer, 2015.

An essential starting point for an overview of medievalism.

McFate, Sean. *The Modern Mercenary: Private Armies and what they Mean for World Order*. New York: Oxford University Press, 2015.

> Several chapters on neomedievalism and medieval modernity from a former US Army officer who draws links between medieval mercenary warfare and contemporary private armies.

Medieval Foundations of International Relations. Edited by William Bain. London: Routledge, 2017.

> Seeks medieval answers to modern issues in international relations, and resists the notion that international relations can only address the modern period.

Montoya, Alicia C. *Medievalist Enlightenment: From Charles Perrault to Jean-Jacques Rousseau*. Cambridge: Brewer, 2013.

> Establishes the centrality of the medieval to the Enlightenment, especially to the ideas of modernity and progress.

Nisbet, Robert. *The Quest for Community: A Study in the Ethics of Order and Freedom*. Wilmington: ISI Books, 2010.

> Conservative sociologist who traces (and laments) modernity's shift away from idealized medieval communalism towards detached individualism. Published in 1953 and still an important book for the contemporary right.

Pugh, Tison and Angela Jane Weisl. *Medievalisms: Making the Past in the Present*. New York: Routledge, 2013.

> The final chapter on political medievalism examines the primitive, violent Middle Ages prevalent in political discourse.

Roberts, Nicholas P. *Political Islam and the Invention of Tradition*. Washington, DC: New Academia Publishing, 2015.

> Examines the ideology of political Islamists and their reinvention and misunderstanding of traditional Islamic concepts and symbols.

Rubin, Edward L. *Beyond Camelot: Rethinking Politics and Law for the Modern State*. Princeton: Princeton University Press, 2005.

Explores how nostalgia in the Middle Ages influences modern nostalgia for the period, arguing that contemporary political theories are to a degree a mixture of actual medieval political thought and modern political fantasies about the era.

Schlembach, Raphael. *Against Old Europe: Critical Theory and Alter-Globalization Movements*. Surrey: Ashgate, 2014.

Investigates different critiques of globalization from both the left and right, showing how the concept of "Old Europe" has served as an alternative to capitalism and communism that advances primordial European nationalisms via collective memory and shared history.

Siedentop, Larry. *Inventing the Individual: The Origins of Western Liberalism*. Cambridge, DC: Belknap Press, 2014.

Looks at the classical and medieval roots of liberalism and the idea of the individual, tracing a gradual progression of individualism through the medieval period.

Sternhell, Zeev. *The Anti-Enlightenment Tradition*. Translated by David Maisel. New Haven: Yale University Press, 2009.

Demonstrates the importance of the Middle Ages to anti-Enlightenment thought in the eighteenth and nineteenth centuries.

The Uses of the Middle Ages in Modern European States: History, Nationhood, and the Search for Origins. Edited by R. J. W. Evans and Guy P. Marchal. New York: Palgrave Macmillan, 2011.

Studies the impact of concepts about the Middle Ages on various modern European identities and national histories.

Venner, Dominique. *The Shock of History: Religion, Memory, Identity*. London: Arktos, 2015.

> Written just before his suicide in 2013, the last work by the extreme-right white nationalist touting what he sees as the vital cultural values that were refined in and passed down from the Middle Ages. Useful for getting a sense of political medievalism on the extreme right.

Wollenberg, Daniel. "Defending the West: Cultural Racism and Pan-Europeanism on the Far Right." *postmedieval* 5 (2014): 308–19.

> Argues that the "clash of civilizations" theory has permeated anti-immigration discourse and that the theory has been deployed by the far right to shape a common Western identity bolstered by medieval imagery and rhetoric.

———. "The New Knighthood: Terrorism and the Medieval." *postmedieval* 5 (2014): 21–33.

> Investigates the manifesto of Norwegian terrorist Anders Breivik, who describes himself as a member of the Knights Templar, showing how the medieval is used as a vehicle for extremist political ideas.